Qatari Women
PAST AND PRESENT

Qatari Women
PAST AND PRESENT

Abeer Abu Saud

Longman Group Limited
Longman House, Burnt Mill, Harlow,
Essex CM20 2JE, England
and Associated Companies throughout the world.

© Longman Group Limited 1984

First published 1984
ISBN 0 582 78372 0

British Library Cataloguing in Publication Data

Abu Saud, Abeer
  Qatari women, past and present.
  1. Women—Qatar—Social conditions
  I. Title
  305.4'2'095363   HQ1732

  ISBN 0-582-78372-0

Library of Congress Cataloging in Publication Data

Abu Saud, Abeer, 1948–
  Qatari women, past and present.

  Bibliography: p.
  Includes index.
  1. Women—Qatar.   2. Women, Muslim—Qatar.
  3. Qatar—Social conditions.   I. Title.
HQ1732.A63   1984   305.4'889275363   83-25587
ISBN 0-582-78372-0

Set in 11/13pt Linotron Aster

Printed in Great Britain
by William Clowes Ltd,
Beccles and London.

Dedication

To my father, Salah Eddin Abu Saud, who came to Qatar in 1955 as an English Language teacher. Thank you, not for teaching me the language, but for teaching me that man's real wealth is his pride and dignity.

Acknowledgements

It is evident that any book is not the result of the individual efforts of its author, but the collective contribution of a number of people. I will not be able to thank everyone who has helped me with this book, but I will mention the people whose role was decisive in its conception.

I would like to thank especially His Excellency, The Minister of Information and Director of H.H. The Emir's Office, Mr Issa Ghanem Al Kawari, who supported the book throughout; Mr Mohammed 'Abdul Rahman Al Kholeifi, Undersecretary of the Ministry, who provided assistance whenever needed; Mr Tayeb Salih, the Arab writer and ex-information expert at the Ministry, who gave a helping hand during the initial stages. I would also like to express my gratitude to Mr Ahmed Anani, Head of the Research and Documents Section, Emiri Diwan, for his valuable assistance; Mohammed 'Ali 'Abdullah, the Qatari artist, who provided a great deal of help and made special drawings for the book, and also Yousif Ahmed 'Abdullah (both from the Department of Culture and Arts); Mike Startup and Hussein Al Fardan for the photographs of Gulf jewellery; John Francis McCarthy for typing the manuscript and editing the first draft; Brian Burke who introduced me to Longman; Janet Weller for valuable editorial advice; 'Aisha Hassan, my friend and colleague; and finally the man who inspired me with the original idea and the need for such a book, more than five years ago, and who has since been suffering the consequences, my husband, Sultan Russan.

Contents

Preface

Denys Johnson-Davies first came to Qatar in 1952 with an American oil company, which had a concession to search for offshore oil.

At that particular time, he was one of the five people who made up the British community in Qatar. Twenty-nine years later, when the number of Britons in the peninsula had risen to eight thousand, we met during the course of interviews which were essential for my radio programme *Features on Qatari Women*, and which were designed to provide me with the premises for this book. On this occasion, he was just a passing visitor.

We discussed life in Qatar at length and exchanged opinions on the status of Qatari women in the past, then he suddenly exclaimed, "You mean you are actually interviewing Qatari women on the radio?" When I confirmed this, he added confidently, "In Arabic, of course," but I replied, "No, in English," much to the amazement of my interviewee.

To have Qatari women actually speaking on the radio about the different aspects of their position as women, and disclosing the degree of their emancipation was not only a rare privilege, but was also considered a real breakthrough by the majority of the English-speaking listeners in Qatar.

Ten or fifteen years ago, such an enterprise would have been quite impossible, but, at the time of recording my programme and as a result of changing social values, it was acceptable for Qatari women to voice their opinions on radio without let or hindrance. It is worth mentioning here that if a Qatari woman feels she can trust you, then she will be extremely sincere and straightforward when discussing her status in society. If on the other hand she does not, then she will quite simply refuse to talk. It was precisely this honesty and integrity that formed the basis for the programme's success; that is why I owe this book to the women of Qatar.

In addition to this, the status of women in any society clearly reflects the degree of development of that community. That is why it is hoped that this book will provide the key to a more comprehensive understanding of Qatari society and culture.

Introduction

During the course of my career as a radio announcer, I have been fortunate enough to meet several women's groups of various nationalities and cultural backgrounds in Doha. On several occasions my hosts asked me to give a talk on women's rights in Islam, but somehow or other I would end up by drawing their attention to the subject of Qatari women.

The questions asked by these different women's groups were invariably of an almost identical nature, ranging from such queries as why Qatari women paint their hands with henna, to more interesting subjects, as, for instance, whether Qatari women have any artistic abilities and aspirations. Because I genuinely felt that these women's groups were deeply interested in most aspects of the Qatari woman's life and heritage, I ventured to undertake the careful preparation of a radio series that was to be called *Features on Qatari Women*. The main purpose of this project was to acquaint these ladies with the society in which they lived, by imparting as much information as possible on the subject of the Qatari woman and endeavouring at the same time to answer as many of their questions as I could.

The radio series, which was designed by me to be the preliminary stage for this book, relied to a large extent on field research, obtained from interviews with Western women, Qatari women from all walks of life, Qatari men, and in some instances even from some important, high-ranking officials. A standardized set of questions (many of which are explored and discussed at length in the following pages) was developed and employed throughout most of the interviews, in order to obtain truly reliable and representative results. In the same way, the opinions of Western women were examined, basically to discover the extent of their knowledge of Qatari women, and whether the former thought they themselves better off and why; in short, to put all their questions into a clearer perspective, and thereby provide myself with a concrete starting-point. From the very beginning, it became clear to me that the vast majority of Western women had had little, if indeed any, experience of their Qatari counterparts:

> *"I don't really know very much about Qatari women because I haven't mixed with them at all ... We see them go shopping, they seem very friendly, but I can't say I do know them."*

> *"I have been here for twenty-one years and I don't really know any Qatari women. We sometimes visit a Qatari family ... they treat me like a queen ... their hospitality is superb."*

> *"I have lived in Qatar for five years, but I haven't met any Qatari ladies ... I would like to know how they feel about the invasion of Western women into their country. Initially, there was a small number of us, but now it seems there are more and more. That's why I'm interested to know how they feel about us and our different attitudes."*

From these statements, it becomes immediately apparent that some Western women living in Doha believe that Qatari women are kind, hospitable and friendly. And yet on the other hand, there are those who think that Qatari women seem oppressed and in reality are nothing more than second-class citizens within their own society. Both viewpoints would appear to have been based on superficial assumptions, as Western and Qatari women rarely mix or socialize together.

The environmental and cultural differences between both parties make it even more daunting for these women of two completely distinct worlds to understand each other, so perhaps a brief acquaintance with the Qatari woman's heritage should be a vital starting-point. In the endeavour to explore the various aspects of Qatari women's lives, one should take into consideration the fact that, within their own society, women should never constitute a separate entity or world by themselves. Women are and always will be an integral part of their social organization, and both men and women are the products of their economic, religious and social backgrounds. This is precisely why one cannot hope truly to understand Qatari women and their ways, without having some prior knowledge of Qatar and the Gulf area as a whole.

It may also be worth mentioning at this stage that Qatar has for years been faced with an important increase in the population, resulting from the continuous flow of foreign labour into the country. This has consisted mainly of Arabs, Iranians, Indians and Pakistanis, as well as the ever-increasing number of British, French, Dutch, Americans and other nationalities too numerous to mention. Strangely, this large Western presence has had a negligible effect on the process of social change in Qatar, because Qataris cherish their customs and fear the swamping of Arab traditions by Western influences. As we have already observed, the various Western communities in Qatar lead a separate existence in which they have their own clubs, parties and social gatherings. Very rarely do Westerners and Qataris come into direct social contact, the cultural barriers being too great for the former to join the latter in their ways. Of course, all this may be liable to change in time, but in the past there existed a distinct inability among Western and Qatari societies to communicate with each other on a large scale.

Possibly because of this lack of contact, perhaps out of sheer curiosity or indeed whatever the reasons, many Western women are genuinely interested in what the Qataris think of them. In order to provide a brief insight into the content of this book, here are three Qatari university students furnishing us with their own untainted views on Western women's liberation, each reflecting the different ways of thinking on this subject:

> *"The European woman fought for her freedom,*
> *but nowadays we find that she wants to go back*
> *as before. She wants to be at home with her*
> *children, so she's not using her freedom. It is true*
> *that here women are educated and go to work, but*
> *there's still a limit . . . not like European women."*
> FATIMA MOHAMMED

> *"I think Western women have more freedom now*
> *than they ever did . . . they can go to work*
> *anywhere with no objections from the husband or*
> *family, and I think this is because there are no*
> *customs for them."*
> 'AIDAH MOHAMMED

> *"I have visited Europe many times, and I think*
> *that people there live a completely different life to*
> *ours, and none of us will approve of that life,*
> *especially old people, because to us, Europeans or*
> *Westerners live a very strange life. They have too*
> *much freedom. They think we can live like them*
> *. . . but we can't."*
> AMINA DARWISH

From the interviews with many Qatari women, it transpired that their views on their Western counterparts stressed a previously-mentioned fact: that Qatari women believe they understand Western ways, but do not necessarily agree with them. They are still very much attached to their customs and traditions. This does not forcibly imply that they are against change, as for years now Qatar has been attempting to build the economic structures of a modern society; they are merely suspicious of too much change in too short a time. This is precisely why they are against "imitating the West", a social taboo in many Gulf and Arab societies.

And yet why, Western readers may wonder, do Arabs consider Western ways as being taboo? Obviously, certain misconceptions exist on both sides, and the present lack of understanding of each other's social background, deplorable as it may be, is at the heart of such a situation. Hence, Western women are considered as being morally "loose" because they wear revealing clothes, something that just is not acceptable according to Islam or the prevailing traditions. This is but one example illustrating the various misunderstandings between East and West. Despite innumerable efforts to clarify the situation, some Arab and Western writers advocate the theory that East and West will never meet, as a result of the disparities in culture, traditions, religion, etc. If we were to postulate such suppositions, then comparing the woman's position in the Arab world with that of her counterpart in the West would be quite senseless, weighed down with shortsighted conclusions.

Nevertheless, it would appear to be perfectly true that the tradition of comparing Arab women, implicitly or explicitly, with Western women reflects the general pattern prevailing in both East and West when the issue contested is "who is better off than who". This question I propose to avoid, as it is of little relevance to the book.

Comparisons between Qatari and Western women are made neither to prove the superiority of one or the other, nor to reveal the similarities that sometimes exist. Rather, such analogies serve the more concrete purpose of clarifying the ideas, customs and traditions of the East, in a style which I hope the Western reader's way of thinking will find appealing and enlightening. Such comparisons were quite successful on the radio series. I still vividly recall the British lady who, after hearing a programme on the *batula* veil, told me that she could understand and respect this particular Qatari tradition; she added that in England older women (her mother included) would never go out into the street or to market without a scarf covering the head. In this instance, the similarity stems from the identical concept of "maintaining the woman's respectability in public places". The strict adherence to such a tradition depends entirely on the circumstances (be they social or historical) of the community in question.

On the whole, the radio series was quite successful amongst the expatriate audience, which listens regularly to the English Service of Radio Qatar. The reaction of Qataris was equally enthusiastic, though the series attracted mainly educated young men and women. They all expressed gratitude and pride that such a programme was locally produced, and the reaction from the Engineering Department of Qatar University was particularly encouraging.

Comparisons can also only be made when taking into consideration the stage of social change of each society. Thus, it would only be logical to compare the Qatari woman in the current transitional society with the Western woman when she was at the same juncture in the process of development.

One final word: the basic aim of this book is to

acquaint Western readers with the Qatari woman, past and present. It is *not* an academic study, and was never meant to be one. That is why the selected subjects are the most controversial.

CHAPTER ONE

The Dawn of a New World

Qatar in the past

Until ten years ago, the Gulf area was largely unknown to the Western layman. The region was just emerging from centuries of isolation, oblivious to the intricacies of world politics, economics and strategy. And yet in the relatively short space of one decade an unprecedented shift took place, and the Gulf is now in the forefront of Arab and world politics. As a result of this, the West has been scrutinizing its actions, more often than not interpreting them in a way that is neither relevant nor does justice to the Gulf's social organization. Many Western writers capitalized on the new-found interest, producing the most unfavourably distorted images of Gulf Arabs. More recently, however, the Western media have shown an honest desire to provide a more objective analysis of the various Gulf societies, and this has proved to be far more interesting than concocted projections. Certainly, the entire area has been thrown into a world completely different from the one it knew; the "future shock" it experienced has not been encountered by any other region in recent history.

There has been a great deal of speculation by the Western media about Westernization in the Gulf. Modern technology is, of course, an essential prerequisite for a sound economy and high standards of living. Admittedly, this has had to be imported, but so-called Western influences and the role these have played in modernizing the Gulf have been grossly exaggerated. Modernization in the Gulf began after its independence, when the local populace was left to look after its own interests in the way it saw fit, and Qatar's achievements since it became an autonomous state in 1971 are further evidence to the fact that modernization is hardly synonymous with Westernization.

If this modernization is a long process largely dependent upon active social as well as economic factors within the society concerned, Western presence in the Gulf never encouraged development. Quite the contrary: in many instances it actually retarded any substantial progress. The external powers who intervened in the Gulf's affairs did not maintain a presence in the region because they wished to modernize it. Their interest was purely selfish, and they kept the area as isolated and backward as they could. The Gulf has long been a strategically important waterway, and the region witnessed great rivalry between various European countries, notably Portugal, Holland, France and Britain. During most of the sixteenth century, the entire Gulf came under Portuguese influence, and its presence was marked by a hostile and violent attitude toward the locals. The latter part of the eighteenth and early nineteenth centuries, when Britain was carving out a huge empire, saw the growth of British interests in the Gulf as a means of protecting her valuable trade route to India.

Towards the end of the nineteenth century, the

Gulf was prey to considerable wrangling between the rival powers, each anxious to gain a footing in the region. In 1895 the French, who enjoyed a strong position in Muscat, wanted to establish a port which could provide ships with necessary fuel. The Germans and Russians were also attempting to exert influence in the area, but remained unsuccessful. 1913 saw the demise of the Ottoman Turks, mainly as the result of a resurgence of Wahhabism into the forefront of Gulf politics and the unratified Anglo-Turkish convention of July 19th, whereby the Ottoman Empire renounced all claims to Qatar. The year 1913 is considered by Rosemarie Zahlan, author of *The Creation of Qatar*, as the turning-point in Qatar's history, marking the end of an era and ushering in a new and totally different situation, "where Qatar was well on the way to forming two new relationships that cancelled and replaced its ties of the nineteenth century with Bahrain and the Ottoman Empire; the first was with the Wahhabis, the second with the British government".

During the first half of the twentieth century, the British presence in the Gulf, and consequently in Qatar, became well-established. But, despite the special relationship that existed between the two countries, Britain never really showed a true interest in promoting important social changes in Qatar. When the then ruler of Qatar, 'Abdullah bin Qassim Al Thani, wanted to build the first hospital in the country during the early forties, the British did not respond to his request for assistance. Moreover, the only modern school in Qatar, which had been constructed at the ruler's insistence, was forced to close in 1938 through lack of funds. The process of initiating development and positive social change was not to begin until 1949, when the serious exploitation of oil yielded 32,000 barrels per day.

When Qatar's oil revenue reached sufficiently high

levels, formal education became the government's primary concern as a basis for the future, and the first boys' school opened its doors in 1952. This was followed by a girls' school in 1956. The political changes obviously brought about social transform- ations, and the provisional Constitution and Declar- ation of Independence on September 3rd 1971 fore- shadowed the changes that were about to be effected in the economic and social orders.

Before the discovery of oil and the improvement in the living conditions which subsequently followed, people in the Gulf led a settled or semi-settled existence on its shores as fishermen or pearl divers. The lack of natural resources made their lives totally dependent on the sea, though some did try their luck at agriculture and herding. During this time, most individuals lived on a subsistence economy; indeed, before the oil explosion most of the inhabitants were practically destitute, with the notable exception of a few fortunate merchants. Because the Gulf was an important waterway, commerce flourished, though never on a scale large enough to bring affluence to its poverty-stricken shores. In addition to trading, pearl- ing and fishing there did exist other breadwinning activities: dhow building for instance, and cottage industries such as making simple household utensils, pottery, fishing nets and so on. These cottage indus- tries sufficed to meet the immediate requirements of Gulf societies, but sadly most of them vanished following the oil boom.

As a result of the harsh geographical and climatic conditions of the Gulf, its people are mostly of bedouin origin. Some settled in cities or wherever they could find greenery, while others have remained true to the bedouin tradition. The society can there- fore be separated into three different segments: nomadic, rural and urban. This basically tribal so- ciety consists of extended families, closely linked by patrilineal ties, which have also absorbed many other cultures. For example, in Qatar many people are of Persian origin, and it is estimated that in the 1930s almost twenty per cent of the settled population of this country was Persian.

An equally large proportion of the settled population were descendants of slaves, who were brought to the Gulf from East Africa during the nineteenth century. Slavery was abolished midway through the twentieth century, and these Africans were accepted as an integral part of Qatari society. Many were even allowed to take the former owner's family name. Needless to say, this close intermingling with both Persian and African cultures introduced values and traditions which, in time, were absorbed by Gulf societies. These extraneous influences manifest themselves mainly in dress and types of food, and also in art and folklore. This amalgamation of cultures in turn produces what we can call a typical Gulf form of behaviour, mentality and way of life. Evidence of this can be found in the way houses were built, clothes designed, and of course in the prevalent social customs and traditions.

Qatari women in the traditional society

We have already observed that certain differences existed between the nomadic, rural and urban communities in the social organization of the Gulf. Each group had its own distinctive relationships which reflected accordingly the woman's status within it. Nonetheless, a definite criterion in evaluating women's position in each sector cannot be realistically applied, as a result of the continuous interaction between each class. Moreover, some bedouin did in fact choose to live in cities, but refused to adapt to their new way of life, and even now abide by bedouin traditions. In this respect, it is more important to consider the mentality and change of values rather than the physical transportation from desert to city. This brings us to the question: what was the status of Qatari women in the nomadic and urban sectors of the traditional society?

In the past, most Qatari women belonged to the bedouin sector of society before settling in coastal towns. Through the practice of veiling and seclusion (we shall look into this more deeply in the next chapter), it has been suggested that women in Qatar and the Gulf in general have led a completely different life in a world of their own, far removed from the domain of men. Many sociologists have even pointed out that bedouin communities can be divided into two completely opposing entities: the private sphere of women in the tent, and the public world of men. Such a division obviously implies that bedouin women have no influence whatsoever on the society in which they live. Nevertheless, some recent studies of the woman's role in the nomadic communities of the Middle East have revealed that through her supposedly maternal responsibilities in the private sphere, the bedouin woman has also paradoxically made a strong impact on the more elitist public domain. In private, women were largely responsible for such tasks as taking care of livestock, selling dairy products, etc. Other activities included selling hand-woven rugs, cloth, tents and such duties as purchasing the necessary merchandise and foodstuffs for the family.

Bedouin women were therefore responsible for the process of buying and selling within their own tribe. It is precisely because they were able to shoulder the burdens of such responsibilities that they were also able to exert indirect influence on the execution of decision-making within their own tribe, always considered as being the man's task. Several studies have indicated that as a result of women's ability to run their own society, men could leave their families for

longer stretches of time in search of another livelihood. In Qatar, for example, men went out to sea
on long pearl fishing trips or as merchants, since
settlements in Qatar were established in coastal
areas, yet society continued to function during their
absence.

Despite the fact that women were separated from
men within their special quarters in the tent or later
in the house, they were still able to know what was
going on in the public sphere, either through their
male relatives, salesmen, and visitors, or even from
other women in neighbouring tribes on their way to
collecting wood or bringing water. Thus, despite the
seclusion, which itself is a direct result of the social
structure, the correlation between these two worlds
(women in the private domain and men in the public
sphere) did exist, and in clearly demonstrable ways.

From the various interviews carried out with the
older generation on the role of Qatari women in the
past, people expressed the belief that formerly
women were more active participants in economic
responsibilities than they are at present, certainly at
least where unpaid work was concerned. They played
a major and decisive role in contributing to common
productive activities, in addition to executing the
more commonplace household chores. Even the
younger generation of Qatari women shares this
viewpoint. When asked about their mothers' and
grandmothers' role, one said: "Our mothers worked
hard in the past, and contributed something to this
society ... now it's our turn to do the same." Another
girl criticized the way of life women enjoy nowadays:
"The Qatari woman these days leads a very easy
existence compared to our mothers and grandmothers. We are spoiled. They worked very hard and
had many responsibilities. Today women have servants, nannies and sometimes even cooks. If not,
there are automatic washing machines, vacuum

cleaners, dishwashers ... there's practically everything to make their lives easy."

This is certainly very true as far as the house is
concerned, but the challenges posed by a modern way
of life are not easy and straightforward. Reconciliation between the old and new is the difficult and
unenviable task which the younger generation of
Qatari women deals with every day, and which
obviously necessitates mutual adjustment.

In traditional Qatari society, a woman's life followed a certain logical sequence from birth, infancy,
childhood and adolescence, to married life and
motherhood. This succession was marked by well-
defined passage rites: being taught in Koranic
schools, wearing the veil, wedding and childbirth,
and in some cases divorce and remarriage. Nevertheless, such a pattern of social development does not
apply to most Qatari women nowadays, and in the
past it was mostly true of the urban rather than the
nomadic sector.

In the bedouin tradition, education was of little
importance and scarcely readily available to the
majority of women, who led mainly unsettled lives.
While the man's duty was to defend the tribe,
nomadic women wove or dyed cloth, mats and
carpets, built tents, took care of livestock and carried
out the household chores. This role changed very
little. On the other hand, the urban woman's access to
Koranic education was far greater. Usually, there was
little if indeed any financial reward involved in
teaching the Holy Book of Islam. Girls went to the
house of the teacher, who taught them to read,
understand and memorize the Holy Koran, considered the most accomplished literary work in classical
Arabic. When that had been achieved, usually by the
age of ten, the family would celebrate *al khatma*, or
the end of memorizing the Koran. The girl was then
dressed up in new clothes and golden ornaments, and

walked through her *fareej* (district) accompanied by other girls, singing special religious songs. People would give money to the children who carried a special purse for the occasion. When this was full, the girls took it to the teacher's house as a reward for her achievement in helping the young girl to learn the Koran.

Despite this limited education, women's role in the economic field obviously depended on the social class to which they belonged. Fishermen's wives, for example, sometimes helped their husbands by working as saleswomen in the fish market. The divers' wives, indeed women related to all those involved in pearl fishing trips, played a vital part during the absence of their men. Many have pointed out the fact that the pearling industry was of paramount importance to the economic and social structure of Qatar and the main source of its livelihood. In *The Creation of Qatar*, Rosemarie Zahlan stresses this point when she reveals that "half the population in Qatar was engaged in pearling. Bearing in mind that fifty per cent of the population were men, almost the entire male population left the main towns for the pearling banks during the season".

Women were responsible for sewing and preparing men's clothes for the pearling trip. While the main breadwinner was away, some would even sell dairy products to their neighbours if the family was in need of additional income; others who could not afford to own a cow ground wheat or made clothes in return for money.

The men obviously had to work very hard during the pearling trips. They would set off for the pearl beds (*hayaraat*) and did not return home until the very end of the season, normally during the last few days of September. Life on board the boats was uncomfortable and dangerous. The captain (*nou khada*), divers, haulers, cooks, apprentices and all others involved, lived in enclosed, cramped surroundings, in the unbearable humidity and heat of the summer sun. The divers had by far the most perilous job, often putting their lives at risk. Their nostrils were held closed by a wooden peg (*al ftam*), and they plunged to the sea-bed working their way down an anchored rope, usually to a depth of about five metres. Oysters were collected by hand, prised off rocks with the help of a knife or any available piece of metal. As a diver could only hold his breath on average for two minutes, this was an arduous process. Furthermore, there existed other dangers such as sharks, sea snakes and other poisonous fish.

After resting for a while, the diver had to return to the sea-bed in search of more oysters, and continue until his shift came to an end. Food would normally be eaten in the evening, and consisted mainly of rice, fish and dates. Later on, the oysters were prised open, the pearls extracted and grouped according to quality and size.

The various regulations regarding the financing of pearling trips also followed strict procedures. Whether or not a *nou khada* actually owned the boat, he would invariably have been obliged to borrow money from businessmen at the beginning of the season in order to buy provisions, as well as pay for the actual labour force. The divers themselves usually had to borrow money from the captain so that they could feed their families during their absence. The *nou khada* would charge high interest rates on these advances. When the pearling season came to an end, all the various debts had to be repaid, usually in instalments, including, of course, the interest. The pearl fishing trips took so long because the *nou khada* and the divers themselves wanted a large catch in order to obtain a reasonably-sized share of the profits, and hence ensure survival. Nevertheless, it was the captain who gained most of the benefits, as

the other members of the crew would earn a subsistence wage which would barely cover their debts. The
outcome was that divers became indebted to the
point where they were forced to work off their debts,
which were sometimes inherited by their sons.

An insight into the rigours of pearl fishing trips is
necessary to understand why this class of women led
such insecure lives. Father, husband or sons (sometimes all three) were involved in an extremely
hazardous occupation; death was a risk, as was
inability to support the family following the loss of an
arm or leg resulting from a shark attack. The divers
also suffered from a variety of skin diseases, related to
being submerged for long stretches of time. De-
pressurization was also a constant danger, as this
could cause incurable ear injuries.

All this had a profound effect on this class of women.
As a rule, they were pessimistic and a sad, gloomy
atmosphere pervaded the whole community during
these pearl fishing trips. Any cry in the neighbourhood
would inevitably be interpreted as an ominous sign of
impending disaster. Their attitude toward the sea was
one of intense hatred and stark fear. Superstitious
practices and traditions were thus commonplace. A
typical example of this is found in the various customs
followed when a woman went to the seashore, awaiting
the return of the boats carrying the men. She would
perform certain rites (which are in no way related to
Islam): lighting the leaf of a palm tree and pathetically
trying to set fire to the sea was an evident symbol of
their hatred for the waters. One of the more popular
songs no doubt reflects their innermost feelings:

> *"Enough, enough, oh sea! It's already been two
> months... Don't you fear God? Bring them back,
> bring them back!"*

In the event of the husband's dying during one of
these trips, leaving behind outstanding debts, the

woman might sometimes be forced to make one of her sons work as a diver or hauler to ensure repayment. In Abu Dhabi, there were cases of women themselves having to work as divers.

The minority of women belonged to the wealthier stratum and a few were rich enough to have their own commercial enterprises, such as trading in jewellery, though a man would represent their interests. These women owned wealth and made use of it as they wished. Yet most women belonging to the wealthy sector of society did not own the wealth themselves, but were married to rich men.

The wealthier women did not normally participate in or contribute much to the economic life. The wives of merchants or landlords had to abide by very strict rules of social conduct in order to avoid tainting their good reputation, and thus, despite the relatively luxurious life they led, they were also more or less completely isolated from the world of men. This class of women had to live under the threat of a second wife, as rich husbands could afford to marry more than one woman. This is a religious right which was often abused, as we shall see in a later chapter.

Nevertheless, it is by this last group of women – the minority – that the entire society seems to be judged. Outsiders or travellers paint a false image of Qatari women in the current transitional society, based on this small minority. They assume that wealthy women are still predominant in modern-day society. In the following chapters, this book will attempt to explore such misconceptions, and try to provide a more realistic understanding of the different classes of Qatari women.

Obviously, deep-rooted traditions and customs played the greatest part in limiting the importance of Qatari women. Here is a description of the sort of life they led more than thirty years ago, made by one of the first Western women to set foot in Qatar in 1950.

Aziza Plant, wife of the then British Resident, vividly recalls what conditions were like at the time: "Doha was a big village in which everybody knew one another. There was no telephone, and very few people even had radios. There was hardly enough water for drinking or cooking, and the little there was came from the desert (well water) which we used to boil and filter. There was no electricity, and of course no air-conditioning. Women didn't go to work, and there was no formal education except for the Koranic schools. All women wore the face-mask, called a *batula*, and the overveil. Even the younger girls aged twelve and over were forced to wear the *batula* in those days ... at first, they cried, and the dark blue colour of the *batula* covered their eyes and faces ... after a few days they got used to it ..."

In 1953, Aziza left Qatar, but has continued returning as she has many friends. When I asked her if she had noticed any change in the woman's status, she replied: "Yes, a tremendous change ... In fact, oil transformed their lives completely. They were very poor, but now girls go to university and speak good English, mothers know more about taking care of children ... In the past, they were not allowed to go to the *souq* (market); they used to send the servant to the shops to bring back material, and he used to come and go several times before they chose a piece. Nowadays, they travel to London, France or Germany". We must remember that Aziza Plant's descriptions of Qatar in 1950 are those of a country which had just started to benefit from its oil revenues. The women she refers to came from the upper class with whom she mingled at the time.

Here is another description of days gone by from Mariam, an old Qatari woman who recalls how people in the neighbourhood lived like one large family. Usually, women united to help a friend if she was badly in need of money, food, clothes etc. "When the men were away diving, some women helped each other build houses. If one woman, say, had to build a small room adjacent to the house and found no man to do the job, she would invite her neighbours to breakfast – an indication of her desire for their assistance – and after breakfast she would talk to them about what she intended to do, and they all helped her... But nowadays, it's not like that any-more. People are not interested in their neighbours. They forget that the Prophet Mohammed said we must look after our neighbours." Of course, this system of *al mufazaa*, which Mariam talks about, existed within the whole Gulf region, and neighbours helped each other without expecting any reward.

Mariam believes that in the past women worked harder, but life was easier. "We used to breast-feed our babies until they were infants. We never used *podar* (powdered milk). Nowadays, everybody is using *podar*. Of course, some women couldn't breast-feed their babies, but then other women would take them and breast-feed them with their own. The woman had to ask permission from her husband before breast-feeding other babies. Naturally, she would accept no money. When some babies cried for long hours and were restless because they couldn't sleep easily, we used a palm date which we put in a *shash* (a piece of white gauze material) to make a dummy for the baby.... We had to improvise, didn't we? When that didn't work, we knew the baby must have indigestion, in this case we gave him *bint al dahab*, a herbal medicine ... Arab medicine, you know, and mix it with butter and sugar, and put a little bit on his tongue. For colds, coughs and other things, we also gave a special herb, though I can't remember its proper name now. If they had tonsilitis, a certain woman came to the house. She put some Arab medicine on their tonsils, and tied a cloth around their faces to soothe the pain. Children weren't often ill, like nowadays, despite the climate they lived in.... But it wasn't hot, it is hotter now.... I remember we used to have pleasant weather, but now it's extremely hot if the air-conditioning is turned off."

Curiously, what Mariam says is partially true, not only because people's bodies have adapted themselves to the new, cooler air-conditioned indoor temperature, but also because of the way in which houses were built in the past. The material employed was readily available: rocks and clay to build walls, while roofs were made of wooden poles covered with palm leaves. This, along with small openings in the roof, ensured good ventilation of the house, and the least possible retention of heat. Windows were very small and covered with wooden pieces to let the light in, but not the heat, in the same way as modern shutters. Houses were constructed in rectangular shapes; in the centre a space was used as a garden to help give a cooling effect, and this was surrounded by the rooms. Similar structures can be found in the south of Spain, where *patios* were built for the same purpose. Qataris showed great imagination in constructing their houses to meet climatic conditions. Some houses even had special wind towers which allowed further ventilation.

Mariam described what life was like thirty years ago. Needless to say, these conditions have greatly changed since then, now that Qataris can enjoy the material benefits brought by oil revenues. A noticeable trend in most Gulf societies, and certainly in Qatar, is that at first women led more restricted lives than they did even ten years ago, simply because the oil boom meant that there was enough money earned by the male population to support the family, without the woman's contribution.

In Qatari society, values were reflected in certain ways. For example, a respectable man was one whose wife did not have to work. A respectable woman was one who refrained from revealing her beauty or adornments before strange men and who lowered her voice when speaking.

Women's economic role diminished temporarily, until they began joining the work force in greater numbers during the early seventies. As education progressed, there also arose the danger of an unacceptably sudden change in customs and values. Qataris believe that transformations should only come with the passing of time, and until now have resisted many tempting sudden changes. Altering values signifies discarding older ones, and replacing them with newer modes of behaviour. This leads to a greater conflict between generations, widening an already considerable gap. After all, what might have been considered taboo in the past might suddenly become the accepted norm and vice-versa. A society's institutions and regulations, its codes of behaviour, are designed to preserve such values, and any change must come from within the society in question. Change should not be brought about through contact with alien cultures, imported machinery and all the other industrial paraphernalia necessary for the lengthy process of modernization.

The mid-sixties heralded the time when Qatar entered the transitional stage of development, when the change towards modernization entered a concrete phase. According to Professor Johaina Al Issa, the first Qatari woman sociologist, "the modernizing factors in the Qatari community can be summarized in the following: the development of the economic system seen in the industrial field, especially the oil industry, the development of the political system, and the spread of mass communication".

To understand the true nature of the transitional society, one should investigate how this phenomenon is lived at the individual level. Here is a synopsis of the Qatari woman's role in 1968, taken from *Papers of a Traveller in the Arabian Gulf*, where Kuwaiti journalist Hidayat Sultan Al Salem, writes:

> *Most women do not go out of their houses, except on rare occasions ... they go to the market place once a year. Of course, women are completely secluded from men, they have their own social gatherings and parties. Mixing between the two sexes doesn't exist at all. There are no cinemas in Qatar, except one in Umm Said. Radio and newspapers are the women's only link with the outside world.*

The author adds:

> *... most Qatari young women don't wear the* batula *any more ... they wear a veil covering the face instead ... yet there's no such thing as an unveiled woman. There is one Qatari girl studying at university level in Kuwait. She is the first to take such a step, but five girls will follow suit next year. Older women are anxiously awaiting government plans to open literacy centres for them, so that they can get the education they missed.*

It is probably just as astonishing for the reader to know that this relatively recent description of the life of Qatari women can no longer be applied, as it is for anyone who actually lived through these changes. Nowadays, not only do women work, they also socialize more than ever before. They go to the marketplace either with their husbands or other women, and most are not completely secluded from men. The veil itself is vanishing, and the number of female university students is increasing. On the social level, it was during the early seventies that customs and values began to be affected by the significant material changes Qatar was undergoing. To take a basic example, the number of cars on the road has increased considerably and, until recently, women sat in the back seat while the husband was driving. Nowadays, most sit beside the husband in the front seat. This is almost symbolic of the forces at work, as the status of Qatari women has now moved from the back seat of a limited role, into more prominent, accepted and active presence in the positive development of their society.

How did this all happen so quickly? What function will the Qatari woman be assuming in the 1980s? Do Qatari women work with male colleagues, is their salary equal, or do veiling and seclusion still persist? Do they still marry very young, sharing the house with other wives, and what rights do they enjoy within the family? Do they have any artistic or literary abilities and do they fulfil their professional aspirations? Are the men's attitudes changing with regard to these issues, and if so does such a change have any bearing on the present as well as the future status of Qatari women? These questions will be fully discussed in the following chapters.

CHAPTER TWO

The Veil and the Batula

"Equal in spirit, but not in society" is the caption of a picture of a veiled woman which appeared in an article on Islam in the January 1981 edition of *The Economist*. This is just one of many similar essays, where the Western media consider the veil as the symbol of Arab and Muslim women's suppression or backwardness. Is such a projection the result of present misunderstandings between the different cultures of East and West, or is it rather a misrepresentation of such issues – whether intentional or not – by the Western media? Could it, on the other hand, be a true reflection of the woman's status in Arab societies? What concerns us here is not the veil in itself, but rather what lies beyond it, both in the symbolic and sociological spheres of interest.

The West sees the veil as a well-established religious practice, which indicates a Muslim woman's lowly position in her society. Naturally, the veil is still accepted as a fashion in the West, and people still agree with certain forms of veiling in marriage, church ceremonies and funerals. The practice of veiling in the East is basically a social institution with pre-Islamic roots. Of course, one could argue that by its very nature any religion forms an integral part of the relevant society's culture. This is especially true of Islam, which has exercised an all-important role in developing the various aspects of Arab culture. Nevertheless, even the most orthodox and conservative of Muslim scholars have conceded that some of the traditions most commonly attached to Islam are either social rather than religious fabrications, or pre-Islamic customs which were not discarded because of the usefulness or importance they eventually assumed. As far as we are concerned the veil is the most outstanding example of this.

In this chapter, we will look into the origins of the veil, its religious bearing, the social factors which made the *batula* a form of veiling identified with the Gulf area and a basic necessity. I shall discuss whether or not it has a future in relation to the new trends which affect young Qatari women. But, in order to avoid confusing people who know little about the subject, we must begin by differentiating between the various and totally different types of veil, each particular to one region of the Arab world.

Types of veil

What people understand by a "veil" in Muslim or Arab culture is not necessarily shared by their Western counterparts. For the latter, the veil is a form of head cover, normally concealing the hair or lower part of the face, while the Muslim interpretation differs in the sense that a veil may completely hide a woman's countenance. In both cultures, however, the permutations are numerous, and in the past Western women sometimes wore the fashionable veil which covered the entire face, while nowadays many Muslim women are resorting to the veil which covers the hair but reveals the face, closely resembling a nun's habit. The *batula* is the veil traditionally worn in Qatar, and I use the word "veil" very loosely because it is in fact a face mask which conceals the whole face, though it does have two slits for the eyes.

Until a few decades ago in most Arab countries women wore a veil which either covered the face completely, or only revealed the eyes. The actual veil consists of several parts, each serving a different purpose and having a different name.

First, there exists the veil which covers the face completely – *al hijab*, locally called *bo'shiya*. This is a translucent or transparent piece of cloth almost a metre long and half a metre wide. It covers part of the head and is placed under the overveil to stretch over the woman's face until it almost reaches her waist. *Al niqab* is the Arabic name for the veil that covers the nose, chin and neck, and is attached to the head cover, while *al qina'* (mask) refers to the veil that hides most of the face and only reveals the eyes. *Al burqu'* is another type of veil that hangs from the head down to the shoulders with openings for the eyes. This, in fact, is the bedouin veil, which is locally known as *al magroon*.

The *magroon*. The veil worn by bedouin women.

Finally, *al khimar* is the Arabic name sometimes wrongly given to the previously mentioned types of veil. *Al khimar* is really a head cover hanging over the shoulders, neck and part of the forehead, closely resembling a nun's habit.

Black veils of this kind were not prevalent in the Hijaz and Arabia at the beginning of Islam, but were probably common in Iraq. Al-Isfahani narrated in his book *Kitab al-Aghani*, that a merchant from Kufa once went to Medina and sold all the veils he had except the black ones. A poet friend of the merchant then composed some lines which translate:

> *Say to the beautiful woman in her black veil,*
> *What have you done to the man who dedicated*
> *   himself to prayer?*

These lines became so popular (and still are) that the merchant sold all the black veils he had, and they became widely used in Medina.

The head cover, *al 'isaba*, is a square piece of black cloth, usually very light, which is folded into a triangular shape, and is then wrapped around the head. Finally, there is the overveil, which covers the head and the rest of the body from head to toe, revealing the face only, which as we have already seen is covered either completely by *al hijab*, or with the eyes revealed by *al niqab*, *al 'isaba* or *al burqu'*.

The overveil is known by different names in different Arab countries. In Qatar, it is the *'abaya* or *dafa*, in Egypt it is called *milaya*, while in Morocco the word is *gilaba*. The various types of veil were also of different colours. White in Morocco, in Egypt *al niqab* and *al khimar* were white and changed to black, while the overveil was always black. In the Gulf, the *'abaya* and *batula* are black. The permutations were many; some veils were made of net-like material (Egypt), while others were decorated with silver coins (Sinai bedouin) and in some cases were even embroidered (Salalah, Oman). Names of such veils varied from place to place.

An Omani woman's *batula* embroidered in gold.

The veil covering the face was originally made of translucent material, as it was intended to conceal the face of the woman wearing it. Later, women wore transparent veils, and before these died out they wore a scarf on their head. Indeed, some still do, but its usage is mainly restricted to the older generation. Younger women who are now once again wearing the Islamic veil, use a black chiffon cloth which is wrapped around the head and neck but reveals the face. It is common knowledge that Christian women also wore such veils in the Arab world.

Some Westerners believe that the predominantly black colour of women's clothing is another illustration of male prejudice. Men, after all, dress in white from head to toe, a cool, heat-reflecting colour. Black of course is very conservative, and the various overveils serve the purpose of hiding the more showy clothes women usually wear under the *'abaya*. As such, when in public, women can maintain a respectably low profile and avoid unwanted interest.

The veil in the West

In the West, English and European women in general also wore veils at one time, either floating from the peak of a hat, draped around the shoulders or under the chin, sometimes even covering the entire face. The alternatives were numerous and applied almost strictly to the privileged, who wore the veil practically at all times. Eye-masks were sported during the reign of Charles I by ladies of fashion, in order to keep the dust away when riding. The *batula*, a less attractive mask, was perhaps originally intended, among other things, to protect a woman's face and complexion from the dust and sand in the harsh desert climate.

At this stage, perhaps I should stress that it is not my intention to establish similarities between these two cultures, as the veil might well have been a form of dress or fashion rather than a social practice. The only similarity which I cannot escape noticing is the fact that in both cultures it was the *privileged* or those of a high social status who wore the veil. We must also keep in mind that in those days respectable women were not supposed to look men directly in the eye. This is essentially what Islam requires from chaste women of good reputation. The Koran orders believers:

> *And say to the believing women that they should lower their gaze and guard their modesty.*
> KORAN, SURA 24:31

In the early days of the church, there existed a tradition of separate seating for men and women. Later, Christian women wore the veil so as not to distract men from the religious services. This is a practice still scrupulously observed by women in the

Mediterranean countries. In other areas veils are still worn by women: black for funerals and white for marriages, reflecting the mood of the ceremony. Nowadays, veils are not only bridal, but also the latest in hat fashion as well.

In Greece the veil had an important social meaning, and there was a part of each Greek house especially reserved for women. This was also a notable feature of Byzantine life. In other European countries the veil is still commonplace, though admittedly this is a practice which is rapidly dying out. In Spain, for example, until quite recently debutantes making their first formal appearance in society would wear a *mantilla*, a black lace veil covering the hair and sides of the face. A similar type of veil is still worn by old Irish women. In the West, therefore, women wore and still wear a veil because it is feminine, in fashion, respectable, or quite simply because it is the accepted norm under certain circumstances and for certain occasions. So why did women in Arab and Muslim countries resort to the veil, and where and when did such a trend begin?

The quest for the origins of the veil as a social institution is a fascinating as well as controversial process, which makes one wonder if veiling, as has often been claimed, was a religious necessity, and if indeed the veil was really devised by Muslims. By exploring and answering these questions we hope to learn why the *batula* became the form of veiling accepted by and then identified solely with the Gulf area.

Origins of the veil

The practice of concealing a woman's face by veiling is a very ancient tradition which dates back to Biblical times. This is mentioned in the Old Testament:

For she said unto the servant, what man is this
that walketh in the field to meet us? And the
servant said 'It is my master', therefore she took a
veil and covered herself. GENESIS 26:65.

We know therefore that the veil is a very ancient
custom, and yet we still remain ignorant of the exact
form and shape it assumed during the course of the
centuries. Returning, albeit briefly, to the notion that
veiling was strictly a Muslim practice, suffice it to
add that both the Christians and Jews of the Middle
East also veiled and secluded their womenfolk until
the dawn of the twentieth century, thereby substan-
tiating the likelihood that in reality veiling is a social
rather than a religious institution.

A common misconception among Westerners is
that the veil was originally imposed in the East by
Islam. This is quite simply not true, because the
practice of covering a woman's face in the Orient is
known to have originated in Persia long before Islam.

The pre-Islamic tradition of veiling is believed to
have come into existence in the court of one of the
Chosroes, and was maintained by the successive
Persian dynasties. Covering the face at this time was
considered a symbol of *honour* for the elite, commoners thereby being unable to taint the distinguished
character and reputation of an honourable lady by
laying eyes on her countenance. Women who wore
the veil were completely honourable, and therefore
chaste.

Above all else, "honour" is the key word, paving
the way for a clear comprehensive understanding of
the idea behind veiling. If we trace the history of the
veil in Europe, we find that in former times certain
tribes in Hungary and East Germany veiled their
women's faces as a protection against anything that
could cast the shadow of doubt on their honourable
reputation.

The tradition of veiling spread to the Arabian peninsula through its contact with Persia, and was adopted in Arabia during pre-Islamic times, *Al Jahiliyah*, for the very same reasons pertaining to the concept of honour. Evidence that veiling was common before Islam can be found in the poetry of *Jahiliyah* times, in which veiled women were described as ladies of honour. Among the poets who paid compliments to veiled women were Al Nabighah and Al Zobiani, 'Adi Ibn Zaid and Al Shanfari. Uncovering or revealing the face was believed to be an abnormal act, acceptable only under extreme conditions of emotion or duress, as for instance expressing real happiness or following the death of a close relative.

From the literature of the times, we find a great variety of veils in use during *Jahiliyah* times, supporting our theory that veiling was widespread before Islam. There is mention of the different types of veil previously described, such as *al niqab, al burqu', al khimar* and *al qina'*.

Unveiled women during pre-Islamic times were slave girls, and during tribal wars distinguished women would often unveil themselves in order to avoid being taken hostage by other tribes; after all, there was little bounty involved in capturing a slave girl, as her ransom was insignificant.

We have established therefore that veiling was common before Islam. It would be more interesting to formulate a hypothesis as to why it survived, even flourished after the birth of Islam. Why do certain people – not only in the Gulf, but also in various other parts of the Islamic world – maintain or even impose the custom that women should cover their faces either partly or completely?

Islam and the veil

The truly Muslim view on this subject is that a

woman is completely free to have her face, the palms of her hands and her feet visible to the eye, but at the same time should not take advantage or misuse her feminine attributes in order to attract men; both her appearance and behaviour should be humble and respectable. The following Koranic verse illustrates this idea:

> *That they should not display their beauty and ornaments, except what must ordinarily appear thereof.* SURA 24:31.

The underlined words have been generally interpreted as referring to hands, face and feet. Sheikh Mohammed M. Al Shaarawi, a prominent Muslim scholar, explained that a woman can wear ornaments such as rings and bracelets, and may apply salve to the eyelids since hands and face may appear uncovered.

Thus, if Islam does not advocate a particular system of veiling, why do some people insist that veiling came about as a direct consequence of Islamic Law itself? The supporters of this argument insist that when the wives of the Prophet were ordered to take cover from strangers it was meant that all Muslim women should follow suit (KORAN, SURA 24:31). This is the only time the veil is mentioned in the Koran, and leads one to wonder why the wives of the Prophet were asked to draw a veil over their bosom in the presence of strangers. Simply, the Prophet's house was always open to everybody, and hence there was no privacy for the women; every detail of their private lives came under close public scrutiny. As a result, the Prophet put a curtain between the women and the constant stream of visitors, and told them to cover themselves as *protection* when they ventured outside. This is how veiling is claimed to have been implicitly ordained by Islam. But the advocates of this theory tend either to forget or ignore the fact that during pilgrimage (*hajj*) women do *not* wear the veil, even though they mingle and worship freely with members of the opposite sex, and that women who normally wear the veil must unveil themselves during this religious occasion of the Muslim year. Women should also refrain from wearing the veil when performing the five daily prayers.

Nevertheless, the widely-accepted interpretation is that the veil, having first appeared as a social necessity in pre-Islamic times, was later condoned for almost the same reasons that made women wear it originally. As we have remarked, veiling was a sign of honour. The veil became widely diffused throughout the Arab world as a result of the influx of concubines and slave girls during the Muslim conquests. The privileged and wealthy would distinguish themselves from the lower-class chattels by wearing a veil. Sporting the veil was the privilege of free women, but when slave girls followed suit 'Umar Ibn 'Abdul 'Aziz, the Umayyad Caliph, forbade the slave girls to wear it, saying, "Slave girls are not to wear the veil or pretend to be like free women."

It is worth noting here that in Yemen women who belong to the *akhdam*, the lowest category in Yemeni society, do not wear the veil, while upper and middle-class women still do.

So, despite the fact that Islam started a great social revolution by recognizing women's full and legitimate rights and ushering in a golden age for women which lasted nearly three centuries, during which Muslim women fully participated in almost every field of social activity as warriors, poetesses, scholars and so on, these days came to an end as the veil crept gradually into Muslim society.

The battle against the veil

> *Take off the veil, for the veil, oh daughter of Fihr,*
> *is a malady that saps the life of society.*

> *Everything moves toward renovation, so why*
> *should this antiquity remain unchanged?*
> *No command for the veil in this form has been*
> *given by any prophet, nor approved by any sage.*
> Jameel Sedki Al Zahawi

With the growth of veiling, which reached a peak during the Ottoman occupation of the Arab world, Muslim women became more secluded, thus bringing upon themselves the consequent social repercussions and evils. Charis Waddy explains in her book *Women in Muslim History* precisely why veiling and seclusion reached their height during Ottoman rule, saying:

> *Insecurity must have played its part in making*
> *seclusion seem desirable. Only where law and*
> *order prevailed could women safely assume*
> *freedom of movement: and this was too often*
> *lacking.*

The examples she provides give evidence of this statement. She also states that at the end of the Mamluk period in Cairo there were numerous educated women holding various certificates allowing them to teach the Koran and even jurisprudence. And yet by the end of the nineteenth century, after three hundred years of Ottoman rule, women had been deprived of their right to learn. This sad situation continued until the rise of modern Muslim reformers, who since the mid-nineteenth century have been calling for the re-emancipation of their women. The battle against the veil had already begun.

The reformer, with whose name liberation from the veil is associated, is the famous Egyptian Qasim Amin who was the first to make abolition of the veil a public issue, when he published a treatise entitled *The Emancipation of Women* in 1889. Qasim Amin himself had, since childhood, been greatly moved by the sad plight of women which had grown under the weight of custom, in violation of Muslim teachings.

Among his contemporaries were the leading Muslim
reformers Jamal Al Din Al Afghani, Mohammed
'Abduh and 'Abdul-Rahman Al Kawakibi. During the
three decades which followed, women's re-emancipation became the theme of daily newspaper articles,
poems, and the subject of many scholarly works.
Poets such as the Egyptian Ahmed Shauki cham-
pioned unveiling and women's freedom. There were
other more moderate poets, as for instance the Egyptian Hafiz Ibrahim who said: "I am not saying let
women unveil themselves and go round the markets
between men loitering. Neither am I saying that the
veil be imposed as if women were slaves, or as if they
were jewels that should be locked up tightly. Be
moderate; the evil is in restriction or ultimate
freedom."

By the end of the 1920s, women themselves were
playing a more active role in the struggle against
seclusion. Huda Sha'rawi was the individual who has
to be credited with finally tearing the veil from
Egypt's face.

We cannot ignore a most important factor in this
issue of the veil with regard to the Arab world, and
that is the political consciousness of women which
developed as a result of the modern nationalist
movement in the late 1870s. Huda Sha'rawi and a
group of other women had undertaken the task of
distributing leaflets against the British mandate, and
took part in the first women's demonstration against
the British occupation of Egypt in 1919. Many women
followed Huda Sha'rawi's example of discarding the
veil. No sooner had this step been taken, than it began
to be emulated by women in several other advanced
Muslim countries. Thus, the barrier preventing
women from participating in public life was removed, and with the eradication of the veil which
covered the face began the long process of re-eman-
cipating Arab women.

The veil came into being because of *fitna* or the temptation of women's beauty to men's eyes. To avoid such *fitna* (an inner feeling) the veil (a tangible manifestation) had to appear. This visible thing, the veil, became synonymous with honour and chastity, sometimes just a symbol of it. Some Arab thinkers believe that this visible veil is meaningless and that the true veil lies within the woman's self-esteem. The veil should go back to being an inner feeling of chastity and pride with no need for a visible manifestation.

The batula in Gulf and Qatari society

In this section I intend to deal more fully with the Gulf area. Were women in Qatar, for example, subjected to the same social and political pressures, or was the situation altogether different? Why was the *batula* face mask kept alive in this part of the world for longer than expected? What were the underlying sociological and historical reasons for this?

To begin with, we must remember that the Gulf area has only recently emerged into the international scene following centuries of isolation. This region remained almost untouched by Western influence until the twentieth century, except during the Portuguese invasion in the sixteenth century. This isolation is of great significance as it helped tribal customs and traditions to remain in control of many aspects of life in the area. This does not necessarily mean to say that, had the situation been different, a closer relationship with the West would have positively affected the wearing of the veil. The pattern and motivation behind women's emancipation in the East has always been different from and unrelated to that in the West. The strong sense of independence voiced by leading women in the Arab world and further afield, emphasizes the importance of recognizing their advancements as no mere copy of Western progress in similar matters. Arabs are not in favour either of jeopardizing their roots, or of losing their identity.

Qatar maintained its identity despite its strategic position midway between Basra in Iraq and Ras Masandam in Oman, which facilitated mixing and establishing relations with neighbouring countries. The actual geographical location of Qatar, moreover, always helped its individuals maintain their liberty throughout the ages – its proximity to the Empty Quarter in Arabia, for example, meant that the tribes living in Qatar could vanish into the desert when attacked by an aggressor.

Qatari society, like other Gulf and Arab societies, was basically comprised of several tribal communities each held together as a functional entity by a traditional sentiment of blood and unity, and by the recognition and exercise of certain mutual obligations, social duties and rights. In this ethnic society, *honour* was the determining factor of the tribe's status, and the chastity of its women was the embodiment of this honour. This concept of honour is true of all Arab societies, and is not only limited to the Gulf region. We have already mentioned that wearing the veil was a custom which stemmed from the idea of remaining honourable.

Nevertheless, one should not forget that the veil was originally an urban custom; in a tribal community women enjoyed relative freedom, and did not necessarily cover their faces. But when the bedouin women moved to the city, they – as was the case with other city dwellers – had to be veiled because they mingled with strangers from other tribes, or even complete foreigners.

Hitherto there has been a great deal of research into the movement and settlement of tribes in Qatar. Although there is room for speculation, it seems that one particular tribe, the Al-bu-'Aynayn, built the villages around the modern-day Doha area, and it would not be absurd to suppose that this must have been the case with other villages and towns in the peninsula. In *The Creation of Qatar*, Rosemarie Zahlan writes:

> When the chief British representative in the Gulf,
> the Political Resident Lt. McLeod visited Doha in
> early 1823, he found its inhabitants and their
> headman, Bahur bin Jabran of the Al-bu-'Aynayn
> tribe.

Although in the past the country was inhabited by nomads, each tribe was essentially one powerful family unit. As such, there was no need for women to hide their faces from fathers, brothers, cousins and other male relatives.

In the nineteenth century, however, Qatar became one of the most important pearling centres in the Gulf, and many merchants from Persia, East Africa and India arrived in the region to trade with the locals. With this ever-increasing number of foreigners, women began using anything to cover their faces from strangers, as a result of the local custom regarding virtue and honour. Some would use their hands, while others drew part of their dress over the face, etc. Needless to say, this was extremely impractical, as there were the usual everyday chores to carry out, and it was impossible for a woman to carry wood in one arm, for example, attempting at the same time to hide her face with the other. This is why women had to find a practical way of covering the face, and it is believed that Qatari women adopted wearing the same type of face mask as their Persian counterparts, shortly after the latter arrived in the country accompanying their merchant husbands.

Throughout the ages, trading communities have always attracted the attention and presence of people alien to that society. When this occurs, the natives will impose certain strictures on women in order to maintain their virtue, faithfulness and the family's honour. Hence for example face-covering and no social intercourse between women and strangers. This was made possible by building high walls around the house and a *majlis*, a room where male guests could be received and entertained without seeing any of the female residents. Sometimes, there would even be two entrances to the house, one for men and another for women.

Another significant social factor which helped maintain the wearing of the veil for so long concerns the actual economics of the area. As we have re-marked, in order to earn a modest living and sustain a large family, the male members of the community would go out to sea on pearl fishing trips for a period sometimes exceeding six months. Women and children would be left behind practically on their own, as they were no longer living under the immediate protection of male members of the tribe. In many communities when men are away from their homes for long periods of time, the most stringent social restrictions are imposed on women during their absence in order to ensure the family's good and respectable name.

Many Westerners may be astonished or even shock-ed by these social values. But they should not forget that the knights and lords who embarked on the Crusades are believed to have imposed even greater, more cumbersome restrictions on their women while they were away by locking them up in chastity belts. Neither has the circumcision of women, a custom in Africa and parts of Egypt, ever been practised in Qatar.

The batula – shape and design
As we have seen, the *batula* is a form of veiling that was widely used in Qatar. It is a face mask made of a

special kind of leather-like cloth brought over from India. This has led many Qataris to speculate that the *batula* itself originated in India. The actual cloth is dyed several times in a navy-blue dye (*neel*) which gives the mask a dark blue colour with golden highlights. This surface is sometimes gently scraped off to give the *batula* its predominantly black colour. The *batula* which is locally called '*al burqu'*, even though it is a *qina'* (mask), is not on sale in the shops of the *souq*, because the sewing is done by certain women in their homes. As is the case with a made-to-measure dress, the *batula* is sewn according to each woman's individual wish: either with wide openings for the eyes and very short, revealing part of the nose and chin (very much the trend nowadays with the few young women who still wear it), or else with narrow slits for the eyes, the nose and chin being completely covered, as favoured by older women.

The traditional Qatari *batula* and overveil, '*abaya*.

A small piece of wood is usually inserted in the middle, following the ridge of the nose, to ensure that the mask retains its good texture, design and rigidity. This also facilitates breathing. The inside of the *batula* is usually lined with special tissue paper, to prevent the dye from staining the face in humid

weather. It is tied to the back of the head by a cord of
gold braid. The *batula* was an indoor as well as an
outdoor veil.

The trend of sewing and selling the *batula* in
private houses has its origins in earlier times, when
women were not allowed to go to the market-place.
Even the face mask has suffered the effects of infla-
tion; more than twenty-five years ago, it was relatively cheap at 2 *riyals*, but nowadays the price ranges
between 25 and 50 *riyals* per mask. There did exist a
more expensive face mask, *burqu' al reesi*, which was
worn by rich women on special occasions, but this
has not been used for at least two decades and can
now only be found in the Qatar National Museum.
The *burqu' al reesi*, was decorated with small twenty-
one-carat gold adornments, engravings extolling the
attributes of God or the Prophet Mohammed. The
burqu' al reesi is obviously an improvisation on the
bedouin *burqu'* which used to be decorated with
silver adornments completely covering the forehead.
Bedouin women in Sinai still wear a similar – though
longer – *burqu'*, which hangs down as far as the waist
and is completely covered with silver adornments.

The *burqu'* worn by bedouin women in Sinai where
decorations and ornaments are attached to the veil covering
the mouth.

Apart from this, there was no special status attached to the *batula*. The material and design were invariably the same, though upper class women usually wore a brand-new *batula* to each social occasion, sometimes with more ornate designs of gold braid.

In addition to the *batula*, married Qatari women wore a head-cover called a *milfa'*, made of black gauze studded with gold or silver metal squares. The more decorative designs were worn by richer women; being hand-embroidered they were more costly. Wearing the *milfa'* without the *batula* is now the latest trend, especially among middle-aged and younger women. The *milfa'* is worn both indoors and outdoors by women wearing the *batula*, mostly outdoors by younger women.

Outdoors, women still wear the overveil, *'abaya*, usually made of black silk. In the past, it was decorated with gold braid at the seams, but this is no longer the case. Young Qatari women do not cover themselves completely in the *'abaya*, but wear it casually, sometimes as a shawl, or just carry it neatly folded on their arm wherever they go. All this would imply that the *'abaya*'s importance is waning.

Origins of the batula design

References, facts and figures on the origins of the *batula*'s design are difficult to obtain. But we have already observed that *al qina'*, a face mask, was among the types of veil in widespread use in pre-Islamic Arabia, mentioned in the literature of the time. So was *al burqu'*. The *batula* could be a variation of the traditional bedouin veil (*al magroon*), which reveals the eyes but covers the rest of the face. The only difference lies in the cloth used for each. The *batula* had an almost identical appearance to the *magroon* when it was long enough to cover the chin and then it was called *b'gara*. At a later date it was

made shorter to reveal the lower half of the face. Such
a transformation was probably effected in order to
facilitate its use (for example, when eating and
drinking), as women were forced to wear the mask for
longer and longer stretches of time.

While interviewing some Qatari women on this
subject, they came up with some interesting answers
and ideas. One suggested that the *batula* assumed this
shape because women wore it when they accompanied men to war, another hinted that it could
have been designed this way just to scare the Portuguese away! Research into the history of Qatar and
the Gulf area has revealed that the Portuguese, who
came to the region during the sixteenth century, were
almost inhuman to the locals, believing that the
atrocities and injustices they inflicted on women and
children were their religious duties.

Many women thought the *batula* originated in
India, but we know that face masks are not worn in
India. Moreover, the importing of material from
India only started at the end of the nineteenth
century, when the veil was already well-established
in the Gulf. One old Qatari woman maintained that
the *batula* came from Iran.

It would seem that the *batula* could have come to
the Gulf as a result of the continuous interaction
between it and the neighbouring countries. The only
related literature can be found in a book entitled *Siraf*
in which the author, Gholam Riza Ma'soumi, studies
the history of the city of Siraf in Iran, also describing
women's dress and face cover. The illustrations she
provides of a face mask are those of a *batula*. This
book was published in Persian during the early fifties,
and included contemporary pictures of women wearing the *batula* in Bandar Tahri, the modern name of
Siraf.

Sir Arnold T. Wilson wrote that old Siraf is said to
have been established by Kei Kaus, a contemporary

of David, from Kayanian descent, and the ruins support the possibility that Siraf was indeed inhabited during pre-Islamic times. Travellers to the area in the Middle Ages described Siraf as being the most important commercial centre in the Gulf, and the largest Persian port. During the tenth century, Siraf rivalled Basra, the famous port in Iraq. However, the eleventh century saw a change in the fortunes of Siraf, and the city was more or less completely destroyed by the beginning of the thirteenth century. This evidence lends credence to the possibility that the *batula* was originally a Persian form of face covering, and, with time, expanded into the Gulf area. I checked on the validity of such a hypothesis with some Iranians who work at the Qatar Radio Station. They all agreed that the *batula* is still worn in places like Bandar Abbas, Ahwaz, Abadan, Lingeh and Bosheer. They also stressed that *batula* is not a Persian word and that they usually called it *al niqab*.

The *batula* worn by women in Bandar Tahri and Bandar Abbas, Iran, where it is called *al niqab*.

The word *batula* itself does not mean anything in Arabic. In the Arabic dictionary *Mu'jam Al Munjid* the only relevant root is "ba'ta'la" which means: make something definite from other things. Here it could mean: define the eyes from the rest of the face.

Is veiling still a social necessity?

It is a noticeable trend that the upper classes in the various societies we have mentioned were the ones who actually started the vogue of wearing the veil. Nowadays, with education and new work opportunities, it is the very same classes who are discarding the veil, while the lower and rather poorer classes maintain its use. Nevertheless, it would be wrong to talk of women's liberation, since the Qatari women who belong to the upper strata of society, who come from the proverbial "good family", are still restricted in many ways, even though they no longer wear the veil. Any limitations imposed upon them are intended to preserve the family's good name and honour.

The basic point of interest for Western women interviewed on this subject was whether the *batula* is an acceptable form of face covering to the women wearing it? Certainly, this is the core of the whole issue of veiling in the Arab and Muslim world. Do women wear the veil because they are forced to by their own men and womenfolk, and why should this be the case? Is it enforced or encouraged by their religion?

When I talked to old Qatari women on this subject, I was told by Amnah Mahmood Al Gidah, pioneer of women's education in Qatar, that the 'abaya is acceptable because it is an Islamic tradition, but not the *batula*. She added that she had no idea from where the *batula* had come. Amnah, who is over sixty, wears the *batula* herself because it has become an everyday habit. And yet when she was young she refused to wear it until she reached the age of seventeen. This was quite old at the time as girls more than thirty years ago had to wear the traditional face mask as soon as they reached puberty or were married. Amnah feels very strongly against the *batula*, but admits that in her time she had to abide by the prevailing social customs, as unveiling the face was considered a dishonourable act.

Anisa Darwish, another of my Qatari interviewees, represents a different age group. She is in her thirties, does not wear a *batula*, never has done and works as a lecturer at Qatar University. Anisa says, "This mask is worn by old ladies only. It's not basically Islamic, although Islam does stipulate that women should wear respectable clothes in public ... that is why we still wear long dresses and cover the head with the 'abaya."

'Attiga Sa'ad, who is in her twenties, comes from a humble family and works as a telephone operator. She puts her views on the *batula* into practice. As a married woman who does not live in the city, she used to wear the face mask, but discarded it as soon as she commenced work, despite the fact that most of her colleagues were men.

In Qatar University, most of the female students interviewed stressed that the *batula* is nothing more than a tradition. In the eyes of Western women living in Qatar, it is considered a very outdated tradition. Many feel that the *batula* must be rather inconvenient and especially uncomfortable during the hot and humid summer months. Some even believed that men found the face mask attractive. This, of course, was never the purpose of the veil and overveil, which in reality were designed to give women more freedom in a man's world, where they could be seen and yet remain not completely visible, thereby not provoking the misbehaviour of others.

Even though wearing the *batula* is not a social necessity for the new generation of Qatari women, I have noticed a new trend, rapidly gaining momentum with the girls at Qatar University. Whilst many dress in the latest fashionable Western clothes, at least one third have reverted to wearing the Islamic veil, a piece of black chiffon covering the hair and wrapped around the neck. This change occurred about one year ago, and when I asked one of the students if this veil had been imposed on the girls, she laughed at the notion, saying, "Not at all ... this is a growing trend in the Gulf, and I think it started in Kuwait." The decision whether or not to wear the veil therefore belongs to the girl, who decides without the interference of parents and family. This headcovering veil is an Islamic tradition.

Finally, when asked if they thought the *batula* was in its death throes, most of my Western interviewees expressed the belief that it is most definitely dying out, though the older generation of Qatari women still wear it. Young Qatari men and women were asked the same question and they also came up with similar answers, adding, however, that the *batula* has become a habit, and that their mothers and grandmothers refuse to be seen without the mask because they have grown too accustomed to having the face covered in public. Nowadays, most women under thirty-five rarely wear the *batula*; it is considered by the younger generation as part of their heritage, a tradition which is dying out as a result of the transformations brought about by the oil age.

CHAPTER THREE

Qatari Women and Marriage

Marriage, as a social phenomenon, still occupies an important place in the Qatari way of life. Different and complicated details are usually all part of the elaborate and expensive process of getting married. Marriage is also the real testing ground of everything that is said about a woman's status in her society. By delving into the religious and judicial, as well as the social aspects of this institution in the Qatari community, I hope to be able to reveal the existing contradictions between religious teachings and social practices, and trace the changes that have occurred in the last decade.

The customs and traditions accompanying Qatari marriage reveal the true cultural spirit of this society. Even though there exist varied definitions for social values, it is accepted that they are common codes of behaviour which greatly influence the actions and thinking of society's members. Such values are invariably the product of one community, and what is socially acceptable in one area might well be unthinkable in another. With time, such codes of behaviour are subject to change, for a varied number of

reasons. Qatari social values have undergone transformations that were a direct result of the prosperity
which brought about the spread and development of
education and all the other changes which modernization entails.

Early marriage

In the past, an early marriage was common practice in Qatar, even though there has never been any
law stipulating a legal age for marriage. In fact, the
whole issue is governed by the Islamic *Shari'a* law,
according to which both parties must attain puberty
before joining in wedlock. Social practices with
regard to this have varied between past and present.
More than fifteen years ago, early marriage was a
tradition strictly adhered to by most Qatari families.
This meant that girls could be married from the age
of twelve onwards. The same, however, cannot be
said of the groom, whose age was of little importance.
Early marriage was a social custom which revealed
the honourable status of any family in Qatari society.
People were proud that their daughters married
young, because this meant that the family had a good
name, and men would want to marry into it. If the
girl reached the age of twenty without marrying, this
was considered an indication that no one wanted to
be attached to that particular family, thereby casting
shadows of doubt on both the girl and her family. In
addition to maintaining female chastity within an
enclosed society, early marriage was also an acceptable approach to inter-family alliances and group
solidarity. On an economic level, it meant that the
girl's future could be secured, thus transferring the
financial burden from the father to the husband, at a
time when people lived on a subsistence economy.

For the child wife, an early marriage obviously had
many disadvantages. One cannot ignore the psychological shock of being suddenly transferred from

childhood into womanhood, motherhood and all that these entail. Early marriage deprived women of the opportunity of going through an adaptation stage during adolescence. Nevertheless, this practice has had to change as a result of the newly available educational opportunities. In 1961 I was in the first preparatory year in the only girls' school in Qatar, the Doha School. I was thirteen years old and my Qatari school fellows were almost the same age. There were twelve girls in the class, and ours was the highest level of education for girls permitted at the time. Most of the Qataris married soon after the school year came to an end. Nowadays, it is very different.

Most of the young women interviewed on this subject assured me that the age of marriage has risen and now averages between eighteen and twenty-five. I myself have met several single Qatari girls who are involved in postgraduate education or in career jobs, and whose ages range from twenty-five to twenty-seven. I have also attended many wedding ceremonies in which the bride was over twenty-five. As 'Aisha Jassim explained, the social taboos on this aspect of marriage are fading away.

Arranged marriage

Arranged marriages are also a contentious issue in the eyes of the West, as they limit a woman's right to choose her husband. Depending on the social status of the woman involved, the modes of marriage in Arab countries differed from region to region. It has now been accepted as fact that women from the lower classes normally had greater freedom as regards marital choice and could exercise a greater expression of their own wishes. From a strictly Islamic point of view, the girl's consent is an essential prerequisite for the validity of any marriage. At no point in the Holy Koran does it approve of parental force in respect of this issue. If a daughter were really pushed into such a bond, she could always take her case to the religious judge.

In the past in Qatar, a girl often did not even know she was to be married until *al dazzah* or the bridal trunk arrived at her parents' house. The bride rarely met her groom before the wedding night, and had no real power of refusal. Even if she had any other alternative, which is hard to imagine in such secluded societies, she would never defy her father's wish or disagree with his choice. Curiously, the other marriage partner did not have much choice either. Normally, he would be a first cousin, preferably from the father's side of the family, although sometimes marriages were arranged outside the family circle. This did not mean, however, that the girl would be married to a man who was not her equal in social status. Qatari proverbs stress such fundamental beliefs, as for example in this one which translates: "The beauty of a dress is enhanced when the patch is of the same cloth" (*Halaawat al thobe roq'ito minoh*). When a girl married a cousin, the question of his being inferior never arose.

Arranged marriages were sometimes very successful, other times a total failure. Nonetheless, they were the accepted social norm at the time; women were conditioned to this from childhood. Love marriages were shunned and frowned upon by Qatari society, and only meant a bad reputation for both the girl and her family. Strangely, traditional Arab communities never accepted love before marriage, especially as Arab literature is well-endowed with poets who excelled in and were famous for their love stories, which often had a dramatic end similar to that of *Romeo and Juliet*. Young men and women were led into marriage practically blindfolded and only met at the end of the long and costly process of arranging the marriage.

In such secluded societies, women themselves

played the greatest role in arranging marriages either inside or outside the family circle. To some extent, they still do. The mother of the groom-to-be was usually the decision-maker in the matter. That is why after marriage, her influence on the daughter-in-law used to be so great; she was the one who had made the choice for her son. Looking for a suitable match within the family circle was judged to give the most favourable results. If the mother already knew the girl, she would describe her to the son, seeking his approval. If the girl was a distant relative or not related to the family at all, the mother would then pay a visit to her house without revealing the intention behind her being there. There was one particularly interesting accepted custom of seeking such acquaintance. The mother or any female relative of the would-be groom went to the house where there were girls of marriageable age and whose family were of reputable name. She then knocked on the door and asked for a drink of water. Everyone knew this was a symbolic request, behind which was the desire to see eligible girls in the house, and maybe choose a bride from amongst them.

This was no random choice. Previous information about the family's status, the girls' beauty and manners was obtained prior to such visits. The woman would usually be welcomed into the house by the mother of eligible girls, who later asked each of her daughters to bring water, fruit or whatever, calling each by her name in order to avoid any mix-ups. If any of the girls appealed to the groom's mother, she would later describe her to the son, and if he in turn was in favour, the matchmaker was delegated by his family to approach the girl's family with an offer of marriage. A period of time ranging from three days to one week was usually taken by the bride's family to check on the groom's financial, social and moral status. When the matchmaker returned, an answer was usually ready. If they said the girl was too young, or that her elder sister had to be married first, this was a polite refusal. But if they agreed, they would then make all their demands (dowry, bridal trunk, etc.) to the matchmaker, who then gave the message to the groom's family. An invitation to afternoon tea at the bride's home usually followed, and at this point the womenfolk would meet to finalize all the details and marriage agreements before men took over.

Between relatives, there was no need for such "shuttle diplomacy". A visit by the mother was usually followed by a request from the father for the marriage of his son to his brother's daughter.

To this day, arranged marriages remain part of the tradition in Qatar, although they are becoming less frequent because of the opportunities available for both men and women to become acquainted with members of the opposite sex. The telephone has worked wonders in this, and has now assumed the role of matchmaker in these societies. The opening of new shops and hotels and other social occasions also give young men and women a chance to meet and get to know each other. Finally, the effect of travelling and coming into contact with other patterns of behaviour has also affected the mentality and aspirations of both sexes.

A recent unpublished study on attitudes and values attached to marriage by Qatari youth in 1980, written by Qatari professor, Johaina Al Issa, used two samples of male and female students at Qatar University, and revealed that the basis for choosing a future partner in marriage is different from that on which arranged marriages were sought. Nowadays, young Qatari men attach more value and importance to morality, education and culture in preference to the old notions of wealth, family name and age. Female students also placed greater emphasis on the morals, personality, education and age of the groom rather than on his job, looks and financial attributes. There now exists a completely different set of values which emphasize the achievements of the individual himself, and not the privileges inherited through social status.

The bridal trunk – al dazzah

After the arrangement of the marriage, a period of preparations for the wedding ensues, usually one month. When preparations for the wedding are complete, a date for the ceremony is made and *al dazzah*, which marks the beginning of the marriage celebrations, is sent three days before. *Al dazzah* is the first public declaration of the engagement and forthcoming wedding. There is an accepted custom whereby marriage ceremonies are held either on Mondays or Thursdays because these days are thought to have a certain religious bearing. The Prophet Mohammed was born on a Monday, the message was first revealed to him on a Monday, and he also died on that day of the week. Thursday is followed by Friday, a blessed day for all Muslims in the same way as Sunday is for Christians. Thursday (*yaum al-khamis*) also contains in its Arabic name the number five (*khamsa*), which is usually mentioned to avoid the evil eye. Also, the Prophet and the four Caliphs were five. Thus, on the Monday preceding the marriage, the bride's house is cleaned, carpets are spread to cover the floor, cushions laid out, and coffee and tea prepared.

The bridal trunk is sent to the bride's house, where a small celebration is held to which friends and relatives of both parties are invited. This bridal trunk, which consists of a number of boxes and bags, is carried by several women, accompanied by female singers and percussionists. This festive parade usually reaches the bride's home at around 6 p.m. Everyone then sits down, and the bride's family offer coffee, tea and various nuts and sweets to the guests. Rose-water is then sprayed over everyone and frankincense is passed around, after which the contents of the trunk are revealed to all present. These sometimes include the bride's dowry, which used to be in gold or silver coins wrapped in a piece of white cloth. Usually, the dowry is paid on the day of the marriage contract. Also in the trunk are selected pieces of cloth for the bride to make dresses, some pure silk, some *'abayas*, a small prayer carpet and other items for the bride's wardrobe such as golden threads for embroidering clothes. The bridal trunk also includes the golden jewellery to be worn by the bride on the marriage day: rings, long necklaces, bangles, bracelets, and some smaller pieces of jewellery for the bride's mother and sisters. Also inside the trunk are traditional cosmetics (henna, *doram*) and perfumes (*'oud* and *'anbar*). Other boxes in the bridal trunk, *kharj al-matbakh*, provide for household needs: rice, sugar, tea and coffee, cardamom, sweets and so on, all provided in large quantities.

Another important part of the dowry comprises the sheep, goats, camels and cows which are sent to be slaughtered on the night of the wedding ceremony. The contents of *al dazzah* are usually left on display for two consecutive days, so that everyone may appreciate them. The amount of dowry given to the bride is usually made public as well.

This has led other societies to consider marriage in the Gulf as "marriage by purchase", a dowry system which has prevailed in all branches of the Semitic race. And yet even though marriage has for so long been accompanied by a "bride's price" or a "groom's price", this does not imply that an individual buys a mate as if purchasing a piece of property. Rather, the whole concept had an economic bearing. The origin of the bride's price, according to a contemporary anthropologist, "must be sought in a family set-up in which a young girl was an economic asset to her father's family. The departure of the girl from her own family was an economic loss, and this was compensated for by the bride's price. From the viewpoint of the groom's family, the acquisition of a wife meant the addition of a pair of working hands in exchange for the amount paid over to the bride's family". This could explain the origin of this tradition, but hardly its continuation, where living within the extended family is no longer the widely practised trend.

In his book *The Family Structure in Islam*, Hammudah 'Abd Al 'Ati stresses the possibility that sometimes the payment of a large dowry could be seen as the expression of the love of a groom for his future wife. This is true to a certain extent, but a more realistic analysis of this process is that it forms part of the status symbol practices which were, and still are, part of the Arab way of life. Arabs have always been proud of their tribal origins, courage, generosity and other attributes which are considered as being the most important assets an individual can possess. Throughout time such inward attributes as honesty, honour, and good family name were manifested in outward patterns. Thus, the contents of *al dazzah* were a definite reflection to society at large of the social status of the groom as well as his bride. The bride from a rich family could expect a more important bridal trunk, both in quantity and quality, than a poorer girl. Other customs and traditions attached to marriage, such as large festive parties on the wedding night, also revealed one's social status.

The actual ceremonial side of *al dazzah* is dying out in Qatar. The groom's family take the bags in which the bridal trunk is included, without the accompaniment of singers. Nevertheless, despite the disappearance of this convivial side, the cost of *al dazzah* has gone up to almost unbelievable levels.

Thirty years ago, when the bridal trunk was sent to

the bride's house, she did not necessarily know that she was to marry shortly, and sometimes was not even allowed to see her own *dazzah*. Things have greatly changed now, and to the outsider marriage as it exists in Qatari society offers a strange combination of old and new. I was told by a young man, married recently, who obtained his engineering degree from an American university, that he himself was surprised when he discovered that his own wedding included *al dazzah* in its traditional form. Obviously, this custom has been maintained by the older generation who do not want to discard this part of their heritage. The resistance from the younger generation is weak, certainly when these traditions do not concern the basic issues of life. Nowadays, for instance, married couples prefer to live in a house on their own, away from the extended family, even though this is strictly against the prevalent traditions. Most people no longer attach themselves to the ceremonial side of *al dazzah*, and the bride herself gets a chance to go to the market in order to select dresses, cosmetics, perfumes, and anything she would like to include in her wardrobe. More often than not, she will accompany the groom to choose the gold jewellery. The rest of the bridal trunk remains as it was, though it has increased in quantity with affluence. Household goods were provided in the past for social reasons; people were not rich at the time, and this was to provide for the bride and her groom when they stayed at the bride's parents' house after marriage.

The bride's preparation for marriage

Almost forty years ago, the Qatari bride did not really have the chance to prepare herself for her wedding party, as she was usually thrust into marriage without much notice. Girls normally married wearing ordinary dresses and no make-up. When the groom laid eyes on his bride for the first time, he saw her as she really was, without the things a woman normally uses to enhance her beauty. Nevertheless, she was allowed to look like a bride on the following day; by noon she would be wearing jewellery, a traditional wedding dress and make-up. A special celebration would be held, and then she joined her husband. This tradition died out completely, but the preparations which a Qatari bride had to go through a decade ago are still very much in evidence.

These preparations normally began three days before the marriage ceremony. In the past, a woman specializing in the art of getting the bride ready, the *Al 'atshafa*, acted as a beautician. She would massage the bride's skin with coconut oil and sesame oil in order to soften it, for two consecutive days. This rarely happens nowadays as Western beauty shops provide the equivalent treatment. On the third day, henna, which adds lustre and shine, was put on the bride's hair, after which the bride was bathed. The use of henna is still predominant, and is not necessarily restricted to marriage preparations only.

The Henna Night

The "Henna Night" takes place on the eve of marriage and is a small celebration to which female friends and relatives of the bride are invited. The palms of their hands and soles of their feet are decorated with henna. Henna, or *al hina*, is a small plant of the privet family cultivated on the South Mediterranean coast, though some of its best derivatives are imported from India. Its leaves are dried, finely crushed and then packed. Henna is thought to have the power of healing, nourishing and caring for the skin. The use of henna has always been prevalent in Arabia, and it is said that the Prophet Mohammed advised his daughter Fatima to use it for decorating her hands, when she had no ornaments to wear to a wedding party she was attending.

The henna used for decorating palms of hands is usually mixed with benzine and dehydrated lime, and left to ferment for several hours. Later, this mixture is used by the woman who specializes in applying it to create an aesthetic effect. The bride is the first person to have henna dye applied to her palms and, if she wishes, to her feet. This is normally carried out in one of two ways; either by laying out a design on hands or feet with a mixture of yeast and vegetable oil and then applying the henna mixture to the layout, or by using the matchstick as an applicator and drawing different designs with it after having dipped it into the same henna mixture. In the second method, the hand is usually wiped beforehand with a special kind of oil of roses, *dihn al-ward*, in order to make the dark-brown colour of the henna designs last longer. An interesting and rather simple way of applying henna was once used, where decoration in the real sense did not exist. The bride simply grasped a small handful of the wet henna mixture and clenched her fist around it. Her hand would then be bound with a piece of cloth for several hours. This method sometimes left intricate designs that no expert could hope to match. The other methods also require at least two hours' wait before they leave an obvious effect on the hands. The old-fashioned way was in common use in other Arab countries, but the more artistic designs were brought over recently by Indian or Sudanese women who, as I have seen for myself, excel in henna decoration. These new delicate designs are very fashionable nowadays. Beauty shops in the Emirates cater for henna decorations in ever-increasing numbers. Although some beauty shops in Doha can do them, in Qatar henna applications are still mostly the work of individual women at home.

The Henna Night is an ancient Qatari tradition

which is still very much alive, although brides do not apply as much henna as they used to ten years ago. The style and amount vary according to individual tastes, though most women decorate the palms of their hands only. In other Arab societies – as for instance in Jordan – the Henna Night is still cele-brated, but without any henna! This would imply that the occasion has some other purpose, which is, of course, to entertain and distract the bride on the eve of her wedding. Usually, many friends and relatives surround the future wife, and their presence is essen-tial to provide her with confidence, before she is subjected to being the centre of attraction for an even larger congregation on the following night.

Traditionally, on her wedding night the bride would have had henna decorations covering the whole of her hands and feet. In addition to *kohl* on the eyes, other forms of make-up were also used such as the *doram*, a special kind of wood for cleaning teeth which made them shine especially white. Most of these of course are no longer used, with the notable exception of the Arab *kohl* or eyeliner, locally made by women themselves by burning gum arabic and collecting its ashes on a special plate.

The bride's dress and jewellery

The actual jewellery and traditional dress of a Qatari woman are not just a wealth of art and gold, but also show evidence of the impact of different cultural influences on the region. The bride wears *thaub al-nashl*, which is a loose cloak-like 'abba-shaped dress of fine cotton or silk, thickly embroid-ered with gold or silver thread decorations, usually in floral designs. The embroidery of old *thaubs*, tra-ditionally handwoven by Qatari women, was rela-tively simple: normally vertical stripes of coloured silk or golden threads. Nowadays, most of the work is carried out by men in the old *souq*, using modern sewing machines, or else embroidered *thaubs* are especially imported from India. The new *thaubs* have an added touch of colour, because, apart from gold embroidery, shining sequins and small brilliantly luminous squares are stitched to the dress. *Thaub al-nashl* floats rather gracefully around the wearer, and the wide sleeves can be drawn up over the shoulder and if necessary partially veil the head and face.

These *thaubs* have a wide range and variety of colours and designs, but normally brides wear red and green. Red is the colour worn in India, and hence could be a direct influence of close association and relationship with this country. The green colour is worn mainly by the Shi'ite sect in Islam, who not only dress their brides in green but completely surround them with this colour on their wedding night, as this is symbolic of fertility and growth. As white has now become the predominant colour for wedding dresses, a Shi'ite bride should wear green at least for the Henna Night.

Nobody quite knows where the original design of the *thaub* came from. Even though the 'abba-shaped dress *thaub al-nashl* is definitely Arabic, different forms of embroidery were not known to Arabs in early Islamic times, during the period of the first four Caliphs, when people wore simple clothes. Later, however, following the Islamic conquests which brought greater prosperity and closer contacts with alien cultures, more extravagant and ostentatious clothing became increasingly popular. The Umayyad dynasty (660–750 AD) marks the time when gold and silver embroidery was first introduced to the Caliph and the ruling class, and thenceforth denoted wealth and prosperity. The designs are believed to have come from Persia, and special establishments for embroidering the garments of the wealthy were called houses of *traaz*, a Persian word which literally means "works of embroidery". This embroidery usually outlined the neckline, sleeves, and the front or sides of men's clothes. Women's dress at the time was not as colourful, but during the 'Abbasid dynasty (750–1200 AD) which followed, women's clothes were developed to include a variety of colours and styles, and more intricate embroidery designs.

Traditional Qatari clothes can easily be traced back to this period of Arab history when women are known to have worn loose cotton or silk *sirwal* or drawers, flowing out and gathering to a narrow leg with embroidery or lace. Old Qatari women still wear these under the dress. The *dara'*, too, which is a cotton dress, is still worn by old Qatari women and indeed was also worn during the early period. Even the head-cover *bukhnuq*, which reveals the face and is sewn under the chin, featured amongst young girls' clothes at the time and was in widespread use in Qatar until about a decade ago.

In addition to the graceful traditional dress, the bride also used to wear her golden jewellery which covered her from head to toe. The head cover consisted of a jewel-encrusted centrepiece called the *gub gub*, which was held firmly in place with the help of a pin, and attached to this were various side-pieces, *t'lool*, studded with pearls and turquoises. These dangled down the sides and back of the head reaching the shoulders. There existed a less popular form of head jewellery in Qatar, called *al hama*, which was more typical of Bahrain and Kuwait.

The bride also wore a necklace called *al murta'ishah*, meaning "the shaking", which is a gold collar from which small pieces of beaten and embossed gold are suspended, strung together by smaller pieces, and hanging over the chest. In addition to this, a bigger piece of jewellery, *al murtahish*, "the shiny", is attached to the shoulders, and hangs over them falling to the waist. In reality, this is a massive chain mail of linked solid gold coins, which usually narrows to join a crescent-shaped piece dangling from the end. Some brides also wore a long necklace called *al ma'ra*, which is made of one chain, terminating in a large crescent-shaped piece of gold. The *ma'ra* itself is subdivided into other sections, each with a different name.

The *mehzam* is an embossed and enamelled belt with a centrepiece not less than four inches wide. This belt was originally smaller in size and plainer, but with time more elaborate decoration was introduced as it became more and more popular. The bride also wore long earrings (*shaghab*) each twenty-five grams of solid gold, or else bought other kinds of dangling ear-rings of different designs – crescent, circular and triangular shapes of gold decorated with precious or semi-precious stones. *Shaghab* earrings are like two pyramid-shaped pieces of gold, joined together at the base.

Bracelets include wide golden bangles of different shapes, some of which are studded with stones and precious gems, or, as is mostly the case, with glass. These are called *banjari*, while the cardamom-shaped beads of gold on other bracelets are known as *habb al hal*. *Shmailah* are pyramid-shaped pieces of gold decorating a bracelet. These different kinds of bracelet were bought to be worn after the marriage party, as the traditional bracelet for the actual wedding day is *al kaf*. This is a wide golden band worn on the wrist, studded with turquoise and small pearls, from which gold chains lead to a round gold piece, which covers the back of the hand and is attached by smaller chains to five rings, one for each finger. Nowadays, *al kaf* is usually enamelled.

These are the very basic pieces of jewellery worn by a Qatari bride and some of them form part of her *dazzah*, but not necessarily all of them. Usually, the bride's family request a certain number of purchases from the groom, ranging from two to four on average.

Some people still tend to select the most expensive pieces, such as *al murtahish*, the price of which ranges from 50,000 to 100,000 Qatari riyals, or the *gub gub*, which costs between 15,000 QR and 70,000 QR. The less costly purchases include a choice of bracelets, earrings and small pieces of jewellery. All this, of course, is the exclusive property of the bride, which is why it is called *zina wa khazina* meaning "ornament and hoard".

This jewellery is sometimes handed down from mother to daughter, but in most cases it is sold or melted down to be reworked into new designs. This usually follows the death of its owner. Such a tradition seems to stem from the bride's desire to acquire new pieces of jewellery that only belong to her and are obviously either especially bought or made for her.

In former times, when most people could not afford to buy such expensive adornments, even at the cheaper gold prices of twenty years ago, the rich would lend their own jewellery to relatives, neighbours or friends. This not only represented part of the existing social solidarity, but also stemmed from the religious belief that hoarding gold is forbidden. Thus, to ease any feeling of guilt, people would lend their precious jewellery to those who wanted to borrow it for a while. That is how every bride was able to wear such gold ornaments.

This jewellery used to be of 22-carat gold, made locally by Qatari goldsmiths after melting gold English pounds and Ottoman liras which were used as money at the time. Now it is made of 21-carat gold. In fact, work in precious metals is a very old Qatari tradition, and Qatari goldsmiths were highly specialized in women's jewellery.

According to the general manager of the most-established and highly-reputed jewellery shops in Qatar and other Gulf countries, Al Fardan, most of their sales to married couples nowadays consist of belts (a growing fashion), the *kaf* and other types of bracelet, and *al murta'ishah*, the short necklace. Most brides buy the head jewellery to keep rather than wear. Even though there now exists a tendency to invest in Western styles of jewellery and precious gems, the traditional gold jewellery is still very popular, and there are several improvisations on designs of the best-loved pieces. These however are no longer handmade (the craft unfortunately is rapidly dying out); the local goldsmiths now use special modern cutting and shaping machines to make these pieces.

Interested in these designs, I spoke to Hussein Al Fardan, owner of Al Fardan jewellery shops, whose family has been in the business for many generations. He stressed that all the previously-mentioned pieces are of truly Islamic origin, and have existed for hundreds of years in the Arabian peninsula and Yemen. The tradition of wearing them has persisted in this part of the Arab world, thus continuing a centuries-old custom.

By delving deeper into this subject, we find that Islam did not prohibit women from wearing gold ornaments, and that traditional Qatari jewellery can be traced either to bedouin origins or to various Muslim dynasties of the distant past. The *kaf* was originally a bedouin silver ornament, which was different from recent gold adaptations in that it had silver bells attached to it. Nose-rings are also amongst traditional pieces of silver bedouin jewellery of the area. Bracelets were prevalent in pre-Islamic Arabia, worn by women and warriors alike. Rings, too, were used in early Islamic times, mostly as a stamp. Jewelled head-pieces have been worn by women since Umayyad times. Belts were also made of gold or silver, and drawings of them appear in the palaces of Samarra, which were built during the

'Abbasid dynasty. Earrings existed in pre-Islamic Arabia, but the designs can be traced to Sasanian times, and lasted through the Umayyad era. In her book *Bedouin Jewellery in Saudi Arabia*, Heather Colyer Ross suggests that the elaborate Meshed Collar *Kirdan* (a piece of silver bedouin jewellery which resembles *al murta'ishah*) could have been influenced by the armour of the crusaders who wore heavy chain mail. The crescent shape, *hilal*, a popular jewellery motif with the Byzantines and the emblem of the Turkish sultans is part of the new gold designs of such Gulf jewellery. In short, the jewellery worn by brides reflects a long, well-tried and very rich tradition which fortunately still appeals to people's taste.

The marriage contract

The marriage contract is usually drawn up either on the day of the actual wedding ceremony, or perhaps a day or two before if the future couple are already related. If the groom is from a different family, the contract is concluded months in advance, thereby allowing him access to the bride's house without tainting her good name. In Islamic societies, there exists no engagement of the sort that prevails in the West. The engagement becomes a bond when the marriage contract is drawn up, and used to be irreversible. This has now changed, and an old Qatari woman was very critical of contemporary youth who, she maintained, become engaged by wearing a ring but can break off their relationship just as easily.

In any case, the ceremony of drawing up the marriage contract is called *al maltsha*. In days gone by, the fathers of both bride and groom would go to an assigned mosque, escorted by some relatives, to attend the sunset prayer. The bride's father usually also brought two witnesses with him. Once the prayer was over, they would tell the *Imam* of the mosque that they had a *maltsha*. Having identified themselves, the bride's father would sit to the *Imam*'s right, and the groom's father to his left. Marriage was then contracted verbally. This has now changed, and instead of going to the mosque people visit the *Sheikh*'s (religious man's) house, or else his office and later the *Shari'a* (religious law) court. The tradition of contracting marriage in a mosque is still widespread in Egypt, where the couple to be married may go to one of the renowned mosques in Cairo, Al Hussain, because they feel it will bless their marriage. This does not mean that marriage in Islam is conditional upon officiation by a priest, as no such person exists, nor is religious benediction, though highly recommended, a necessary prerequisite for the validity of the marriage. In view of this, some observers have stressed the contractual nature of marriage; as a contract it cannot be concluded without the prior mutual consent of the parties involved. It is open to extra legitimate conditions and its terms are, within legal bounds, capable of being altered. It is, moreover, dissoluble if there should arise serious grievances leading to an irreconcilable breakdown in marital relations. Marriage in Islam is neither a secular contract nor a religious sacrament, but rather a curious mixture of the two.

In order for a marriage to be consummated and become valid, certain conditions have to be met. When a marriage is contracted there has to be a direct unequivocal proposal, followed by a corresponding acceptance. This must be explicit and preferably oral, though a written form is also permissible. This is not the same as having the contract registered after its conclusion, a procedure which seems to have been introduced in recent periods for administrative purposes. The groom should be of sound mind and able to support his bride, who in turn also has to be of sound mind and full age, and must pronounce her consent to marriage if the contract is to be valid. Because of social limitations, the legal guardian (*wali*), usually the father, represents the bride, and this tradition still persists.

Two competent witnesses are essential to ensure that the bride has delegated her father to represent her, and that she approves of her forthcoming marriage. The girl has the full right to have her marriage revoked if she feels she has been misrepresented. The contract also requires the contribution of a dowry or marriage gift by the groom to his bride. The marriage is valid even if the amount is not specified in the contract, and the dowry is to be estimated according to the customary standards. Most jurists in Islam maintain that there is no minimum or maximum. The dowry might be as nominal as an iron ring, or as high as a hundredweight (one *qintar*) of gold or silver. Nevertheless, in the early days of Islam, the dowry was not the burden on the groom and his family it has become nowadays, especially in Gulf countries. Whatever dowry a man gives his prospective wife, it belongs to her exclusively, and whatever she may have acquired before or after marriage is hers alone. A bride has no financial obligations to her groom.

Islam, therefore, made the dowry the bride's right and empowered her to dispose of it as she saw fit. This was introduced to minimize the element of self-interest and influence of the guardian in his choice of a husband for the daughter. It was one among other changes made by Islam which were meant to remove the control over women's affairs from their male relatives and protectors, and vest it in the women themselves. Yet the social practice throughout the years has been for the dowry money to be paid to the father, supposedly to be held in trust for the daughter. Some parents obviously abuse this privilege, while others spend part of the dowry funds on wedding preparations. Large dowries demanded by fathers have resulted in the reluctance of many men to marry as young as they used to. Marriage to non-Qataris has also increased as a result of this.

The final important condition for the validity of the marriage contract is that it should be widely publicized. It is a community matter, and Muslim societies attach considerable importance to the social ceremonies connected with marriage. Moreover, publicity is the element which distinguishes between illicit and legitimate unions. This was probably why the Prophet recommended marriage feasts, and sanctioned folk music and singing in marriage ceremonies.

Marriage festivities

Marriage festivities usually took place on a Thursday, immediately after the evening prayer. The groom's procession left the mosque and headed towards the bride's house. The groom was escorted by relatives, friends and a group of male singers and percussionists who danced *al razeef*, a folk-dance of simple steps whose basic purpose in the distant past was to celebrate victories in battle. When this procession reached its destination, the men would divide into two lines, separated by a distance wide enough to accommodate the percussionists who remained in the middle. Both lines of men danced to the music, wielding swords. Frankincense was then passed to everyone present, and Arabic coffee distributed. This continued for a while, and then the groom was escorted by women singers and percussionists into the bride's room. This room was called *al khlah*, and was once divided into two parts separated by a curtain. The first part included the bed and clothes, but the second part was designed so that the bridegroom could receive well-wishers, and was decorated with many pictures. Obviously, the separating screen was necessary in order to preserve the privacy of the married couple's quarters, and during those times provided two rooms in one. The groom sat on a mattress and received all the friends who wanted to wish him a happy marriage. On their way out, the men would donate money (*nuqut*) to the percussionists.

'*Ashori* songs were sung by the women, and most of these had relevant themes, revolving round the happy occasion and well-matched couple. When all the social ceremonies were over, some women singers would take the bride to join her groom in their room. At one time, the bride was carried rolled up inside a carpet (*zuliya*) by her womenfolk, and taken into his room. Screaming was an acceptable reaction to seeing the groom and recommended as proof of chastity; people believed that if a bride did not scream when brought into the room, this signified that she either knew the man or was in love with him, which was a disgrace to both herself and the family. Some mothers even went as far as pinching their daughters to make sure they screamed. This old tradition died out completely more than twenty-five years ago, and nowadays the bride is escorted to her groom on foot. In other Gulf countries, as for instance in Bahrain and Kuwait, the bride would be seated on a chair and covered with a large green cloth held over her head like an umbrella, and then carried to her husband.

During the night, the sheep provided by the groom were slaughtered, and women would stay up all night cooking. In the morning, sheep and rice were distributed to the whole neighbourhood. This was called *ojrah*.

The bride and groom usually remained in the bride's house for a period of one week, though it sometimes stretched to several months. There was no such thing as a honeymoon, though nowadays some married couples will travel abroad shortly after their wedding for a short holiday. The fact that the married couple stayed at the bride's house for a period of time had its own special significance; it provided the bride with the comfort of familiar places, also the advice and guidance of her mother as social taboos prevented her from discussing marital affairs with unmarried women. It also relieved the bride from all the household chores, which would later on be her own responsibility.

On the third day of marriage another celebration takes place in the bride's house, known as *lailat al-banat*, or the night of girls, where the bride's girlfriends are invited to see her, congratulate her on the wedding and present their gifts. Naturally, women of all age groups are present on this occasion, and the bride's mother-in-law comes on this day. On the fourth day, women from the neighbourhood can visit the bride between the afternoon (*'asr*) and the sunset (*maghrib*) calls to prayer. The bride receives her guests wearing her finest clothes and jewellery. The festive atmosphere continues until the week comes to an end. The bride and groom then move to the latter's parents' house. In the past, they occupied a room of their own, but nowadays they move into special quarters within the house which have been especially prepared for the married couple, or, as is now commonplace, into a completely separate home of their own.

The bride's procession (*al thwal*, meaning literally transfer) from her parents' house to her parents-in-law's home normally takes place after the evening prayer. Her mother does not accompany her in this procession where the bridal trunk, presents and furniture are all moved into the groom's house. That same night, a large celebration dinner is held by the groom's parents to celebrate the arrival of the newly-married couple, *al hadiah*. After three days, the bride's mother is allowed to visit her daughter and attend the final celebrations. Slowly, the bride will become integrated within the family, assuming various tasks allotted to her by the groom's mother.

The best way, perhaps, to illustrate the strange and fascinating mixture of old and new in Qatari marriages is to describe a wedding ceremony I myself attended recently. This wedding party was held at the bride's villa. Seated by the door was an old woman facing a small fire and holding a *daf*, a kind of tambourine, over the fire in order to tighten the animal skin. This gives the instrument a better sound. The court inside the villa was full of women of all age groups and a few young boys. The floor was covered with carpets, and seats and cushions were available for those who wanted them. The group of women singers and percussionists were sitting in a circle around two chairs which had been especially reserved for the bride and groom. The festive atmosphere was further enhanced by the smell of frankincense and rose-water. I sat on a cushion hoping to get a good look at all the celebrations before going inside the villa to see the bride.

The contrasts between old and new were immediately noticeable. Most of the young girls aged between thirteen and seventeen were dressed in all the latest Western fashions, all beautifully made-up with their long, black hair completely uncovered. The twenty to thirty-year-old group were a mixture of mostly unveiled women, while others wore the *milfa*' head cover which exposes the face, sometimes part of the hair, and hangs down the back, floating out behind the woman as she moves, or gathered gracefully over the shoulder in much the same way as a scarf, falling in folds around the neck. The *milfa*'s were made of black gauze and studded with beautiful geometric patterns of small silver or golden squares. They matched very well the fashionable dresses worn by the same group of women. The older ladies were wearing quite simple dresses, along with plain head covers and the *batula* face mask.

I can well remember one particular woman who was in her late thirties. She arrived wearing the face mask, overveil, and very intricate henna decorations on her hands. At one point she removed her overveil, and to my amazement the face mask as well, went into the middle of the circle of singers, removed her head cover, beautifully studded with silver squares, held it over her head, and danced magnificently to the music, swinging her hair back and forth.

After some time, we all went inside the villa to see the bride, who was sitting in her room surrounded by friends and relatives. She looked nothing like the traditional Qatari bride I had imagined; she was dressed in white, like any Western bride, and was wearing very little jewellery, just pearl earrings and a pearl necklace. It seems that nowadays, even when Qatari brides buy traditional pieces of jewellery, they only wear them on *lailat al-banat*.

I stayed in the bride's room for a while, and in the meantime other women were coming and going, wishing her a happy and fruitful marriage. The groom eventually arrived escorted by his friends and went into the *majlis* with them, and after drinking coffee his acquaintances all left. Of course, the groom had already held his own party for friends and relatives. The couple then went out into the villa's courtyard and continued what had started as a traditional Qatari wedding, but had developed into a ceremony that could have taken place anywhere in the Arab world, the bride and groom the happy centre of attraction while the party continued into the early morning hours. Eventually, the bride and groom were taken into the house escorted by women singers, banging drums, and all the other guests departed.

Polygamy

The Muslim matrimonial system has always been described as polygamous. Islam is said to have introduced and reinforced the practice of polygamy, which is claimed to have been confined to Muslims. In historical times before Islam, however, polygamy was definitely a well-known practice in the Middle East. The Bible set no limit on the number of wives a man could take; King Solomon is said to have had seven hundred wives (1 KINGS 11:3), his son eighteen (2 CHRONICLES 11:21). One wonders if there was a tendency to exaggerate in this matter, and some writers are inclined to take the frequent mention of polygamy in the Old Testament as symptomatic of a general practice. Such reasoning can hardly be corroborated, as the acceptability of this convention does not necessarily indicate that it was undertaken frequently by a majority of the population.

The Christian stance with respect to this is quite interesting. According to some scholars, the New Testament accepts monogamy as the normal form of marriage, but does not explicitly ban polygamy except in the case of bishops and deacons. No church council in the earliest centuries opposed it, nor was any obstacle placed in the way of its practice. For example, Saint Augustine clearly stated that he did not condemn it, and occasionally Luther spoke of it with considerable tolerance and approved of the bigamous state of Philip of Hesse. It is an accepted fact that, as late as the sixteenth century, some German reformers permitted the validity of a second, even a third marriage. In 1650, some Christian leaders resolved that every man should be allowed to marry two women. A more recent precedent was the doctrine of Brigham Young's Mormon sect, which advocated polygamy until the late 1880s, when the United States Congress passed several measures prohibiting this type of marriage. Nevertheless, Christians are believed to have been on the whole far less polygamous than either Jews or Muslims. But one cannot say that Christianity introduced monogamy to the Western world, or even reinforced it out of respect for women, or for social reform. Monogamy had already been the only legitimate form of marriage in the Western societies to which Christianity was first introduced. This was further reinforced by the strong tradition of formal monogamy in Greece and Rome, and also by the fact that Christianity took root among the least wealthy free classes, who probably could not have afforded polygamy.

Islam, which belongs to the monotheistic family of creeds or religions, permits polygamy as a voluntary measure which the individual may or may not take depending on certain factors. The key passage in the Holy Koran, SURA 4:3, where polygamy is shown to be permissible, says:

> *"And if you fear that you will not act justly*
> *towards the orphans, marry such women as seem*
> *good to you, two, three, four; but if you fear that*
> *you will not be equitable, then only one."*

This is usually interpreted in conjunction with another passage, SURA 4:129, where the Koran says:

> *"You will not be able to be equitable with your*
> *wives, even though you be eager".*

Despite varied interpretations, the status of polygamy in Islam is no more and no less than that of a permissible act which becomes unlawful if it leads to unjust consequences. The Koran is very clear in determining that if there is fear of injustice, a man may marry only one wife, and this implies a religious and moral limitation to this practice. In addition to this, it is forbidden for a man to take more than one wife if he cannot provide for them adequately.

There exist certain means of defence for women,

whereby a wife may stipulate in her marriage contract that divorce would become effective should the
husband indulge in certain things unfavourable to
her, such as taking a second wife. Polygamy is not to
be imposed, and if harm or injustice is done to a wife,
she may refer to the judicial authorities for protection
or divorce. There also exist other measures to limit
polygamy, as for instance the "delayed dowry",
where a considerable portion of the marriage endow-
ment is deferred to be claimed by the wife in the case
of divorce.

But under what conditions did Islam make polygamy permissible? Among the reasons cited is the
desire of the man to have children if his wife is
barren, or if she is chronically ill. Originally, it was
allowed in order to incorporate widows and orphans
into normal community life, so that they could be
cared for and looked after. Islam did in fact limit
polygamy to four wives, whereas in pre-Islamic
Arabia the number of wives a man could have was
unlimited. Some forms of polygamy were prohibited
by Islam: marrying two sisters at the same time or a
woman and her aunt, etc.

Polygamy in the religious context of Islam, therefore, is a voluntary course of action which is legalized
under certain conditions, and which in the secular
context of Muslim society might have been and
indeed was abused. Nevertheless, many Westerners
have been preoccupied with the superficial and sen-
sational abuses of the practice. The image of a rich
and powerful *Sheikh* presiding over his harem is still
to this day prevalent in Western minds. Indeed, most
of my Western interviewees were strongly convinced
that almost all Qatari men still practise polygamy.
Most of their questions centred on the position of the
first or senior wife, the limits of her influence, the
rights of children by different wives, women's reactions to polygamy and other related matters. Asked

about the situation more than thirty years ago, one of
my European interviewees, who had been in Qatar at
the time, stressed that women accepted polygamy as
part of their religion, and that if disagreements did
occur, wives would make sure their husband knew
nothing of it. Admittedly, this view would appear to
be superficial, as it comes from someone observing
Qatari women's behaviour on limited occasions.

The views of Qatari men and women were more
representative. One young woman whose father had
been married to more than one wife told me that
women loathed the practice. They tried not to show
when they were upset, but problems related to
polygamy, arguments and fights were all part of
everyday life, especially when children were involved. Children are supposed to have equal rights
with regard to treatment by their father, education,
and inheritance. This was hardly true of real life since
discrimination was bound to occur. All children are
supposed to have an equal share of the inheritance as
stipulated by the Koran, but occasionally some
fathers would sell their property to a favourite son in
order to avoid the *Shari'a* courts. Generally, the most
influential wife always got her way. Asked where the
influence lay among a number of wives, a young man
told me that in some families the first wife was the
most important, handling all the household affairs,
while in other families the second wife wielded most
of the power. In most cases, however, the last wife,
invariably the youngest, was the preferred one and
had all the authority of decision-making within the
marriage system. In this polygamous structure there
is rarely a clash with the influence of the wives'
mother-in-law, as this influence would disappear
more or less completely with the increase in the
number of wives, and the transfer of the whole family
unit into a separate house away from the husband's
parents. Sometimes father, wives and children lived

in one house where each woman had her own quarters and servants, while on most occasions separate wives enjoyed the privacy of one room within the house and had to share the rest. This is perhaps the kind of situation where an influential senior wife was required to organize everyday chores.

The practice of polygamy has been greatly influenced by various interacting factors, mainly of a social and economic nature. These obviously combine and react with other forces, such as customs, traditions and other social values. At one particular time, marriage to more than one wife was indicative of the social status of a wealthy man in Arab society. In Qatar, polygamy could have been one way of realizing the desire for more offspring, as this led to greater authority in the tribal community.

Economic factors also played an important role in this issue. In the past, where most of the inhabitants were involved in pearling and commerce, and when people lived on a subsistence economy, providing for one wife alone was difficult enough. But this very same social organization also led, in some instances, to the expansion of polygamy, where seafarers on commercial trips might marry other women in their different ports of call, or where a diver's widow might marry the *nou khada* as a means of repaying the husband's debts.

Nevertheless, popular proverbs disapproving of polygamy abound: "The house of one wife is a success, of two wives a disaster, and of three wives like a dustbin."

Nowadays the idea that most – if not all – Qatari men are married to more than one wife, is simply not true. Though there are no statistics concerning the percentage of polygamous marriages in Qatar, most of the older generation of men and women stress that the ability to marry more than one wife was usually the privilege of the social class who could and still can afford to do so.

Polygamy in Qatar is undoubtedly on the wane, and there are various reasons for this. Education is changing people's way of thinking, the idea of only one partner is becoming more and more acceptable, and, of course, the exorbitant cost of marriage is a relatively new phenomenon. This transformation can be seen in the viewpoints of young Qatari men. Jamal Mohammed, a devout Muslim, told me that he would not marry more than one wife because he wanted a happy family life. He believed that his children would be seriously affected if he married more than one woman, and he attached too much importance to his children to risk their well-being. Fahd Al Khater said that opinion is changing as a result of education and many other factors influencing a young Qatari's life; the opportunity of becoming more acquainted with a girl before marriage reduces the risk of a failed relationship and the need for a second wife. Most of the young men supported this view, even those who were proud of their all-important male role. The economic factor, as most pointed out, still retains its importance. As the country develops, individual expectations and ambitions grow, and in addition to the rising costs of marriage (dowry etc.) furnishing a house with the latest Western appliances and up-to-date furniture styles makes the cost of a second marriage too prohibitive. The total cost of an average marriage in Qatar is nothing less than the equivalent of £25,000 sterling.

Finally, polygamy never really signified a better life for the man and a worse status only for the women involved. The image of a harem, where all the husband had to do was beckon his wives so they could fulfil his every whim, in the same way as the slave girls in the *Tales of a Thousand and One Nights*, was in reality a two, three or four-sided hell, where women's jealousy and rivalry for the husband's favours and attentions threatened the happiness which a monogamous marriage takes for granted. There were cases where the husband himself would become the victim, when his wives would unite against him for the realization of their own mutual interests.

Divorce

Divorce was one of the most interesting issues to my Western interviewees, who believed that this was an example, like polygamy, where discrimination against women was not only socially, but religiously motivated as well. This assumption stemmed from the apparent ease with which a man can divorce his wife, even without justification, while women are deprived of such rights. Related questions involving custody of children, alimony, the position of divorced women in society, their rights with regard to remarriage and the rights of non-Muslim wives, also aroused great interest.

The seemingly unjustifiable ease of divorce in Islam is thought by some writers to be a direct result of the separation of the sexes and the veiling and seclusion of women. And yet in the West, where both sexes can freely intermingle, and where women enjoy more or less complete freedom of action, divorce also seems to be an easy course to take. In the United States, one of the bastions of the women's liberation movement, the divorce rate is among the highest in the world. The statistics for 1979 revealed that the divorce rate had soared to an unprecedented high of 5.2 divorces per 1,000 of the population. The US Census Bureau looked ahead to 1995 in an effort to predict the changes likely to occur, and indicated that by this time practically 52 per cent of married couples would be comprised of previously divorced individuals. According to a 1981 booklet on marriage making and breaking produced by the British Medical Association, in Britain between a quarter and a third of current marriages are heading for the divorce courts, and ultimate dissolution.

In the Koran, the general grounds for divorce is the ultimate and irrevocable failure of one or both parties to discharge their marital duties, and to consort with each other in kindness, peace and compassion. The major kinds of circumstances which may be accepted in this case have been specified by Muslim jurists; some relate to the husband, others to the wife or even both parties. Basically, the ones that may involve either party are: desertion, chronic illness, insanity, deceptive misrepresentation at the conclusion of the marriage contract, maltreatment and moral laxity. If divorce seems simple because a man can divorce his wife verbally, it should be remembered that revocation of divorce is an easier process; within the three month waiting period or *'iddah* which comes afterwards, a divorce may be revoked twice by saying or doing anything that indicates a desire for reconciliation.

In Islam, the publicizing of the grounds for divorce is not considered crucial, and allows the man to divorce his wife unilaterally. Publicity is not thought to be of any great positive consequence as a divorce can be unrevealed but genuine, or can be pronounced and accepted, but actually false. Jurists agree on this, insisting that disclosing the grounds for divorce is unlikely in itself to prevent the determined parties from terminating their marriage. Moreover, it may lessen their chances of remarriage. As a contemporary scholar notes, in marriage and divorce motives can be very personal or psychological, and therefore very difficult to evaluate.

It is a serious misconception to say, as some Western and Muslim feminists have done, that the exercise of divorce is the exclusive right of the man. Both men and women have the right to seek and obtain the dissolution of an unsuccessful marriage. The channels vary in kind, as some are open to the man only, others solely to the woman with or without judicial intervention, and some to both directly or through judicial process.

It is not necessary to elaborate on a man's right to divorce, as the practice of such a right has been established, but it is important to reveal the woman's rights. Surprising as it may seem, a Muslim woman has the right, like her husband, to initiate and actually dissolve the marriage tie independently. In certain cases she may do so without the judicial court's permission or the husband's consent. This happens in "delegated divorce", in which the man agrees in the marriage contract to transfer the right of divorce to the woman only. Moreover, if the wife is betrayed, she has the right to obtain divorce through the proper judicial processes. The husband's consent is immaterial and irrelevant if she has valid reasons for divorce.

In Qatar, social reality in this respect is more in keeping with the spirit of Islam than in some Arab countries, where such a process suffers from bureaucratic measures which can make a divorce suit last for many years. A Qatari woman can easily approach the judicial authorities, the *Shari'a* court, and plead her case. In many instances she will be granted divorce and sometimes custody of the children for life. Usually, the woman asking for a divorce, once granted one, pays back to her ex-husband the remainder of her dowry and does not ask for her delayed dowry. Sometimes, she may even pay back the whole dowry, return all her gifts and ask for no alimony. This social practice is not advised in the Koran:

> *"Make provision for them (divorced women), the affluent man according to his means, and according to his means the needy man, honourably an obligation on the righteous."*
> SURA 2:236.

When a Muslim woman is granted divorce, she is usually given custody of the children, unless she is considered unfit. She retains custody of the boys until they reach seven years of age, and the girls until they reach the age of nine. The father's right to custody is, usually, when the children are of age unless he is deemed unfit. If this is the case, they remain with the mother. Nevertheless, it is the father's responsibility to bear the full cost of their housing, clothing, food and education.

In Qatar the divorced woman does not live in a house on her own, but remains within the extended family, normally with her father or a brother. This is to ensure that she receives their moral support, and that her children are disciplined by her father who assumes responsibility for their well-being and guidance, thereby compensating for the absence of their own father. Living within this extended family structure provides women with the necessary security on the psychological, economic and social levels.

Nevertheless, the Qatari Government provides for divorced and widowed women, by paying them a monthly income to help support the family. This is being carried out through the Ministry of Labour and Social Affairs, where specialized women investigators (all Qatari) look into each case separately, to make sure that the woman in question really is divorced and in need of Government assistance. These women investigators also check the requirements of each divorced woman, and advise them on ways of solving their financial problems. The Government also provides housing facilities for these women, if they want them. In 1975 a special training centre for the divorced and widowed was established by the Ministry of Labour and Social Affairs.

The rights of non-Muslim women divorced from Qataris aroused many suspicious questions among my Western interviewees. Do they enjoy the same rights as Qatari women? Is a non-Muslim wife allowed custody of her children? In order to answer these questions truthfully, I spoke to the *Shari'a* judge in Doha, who underlined the fact that such women do enjoy the same rights, not only in theory but most definitely in practice as well. He added that such cases often arise, and that the non-Qatari woman has the right to custody of her children outside Qatar, and that the woman who takes her offspring to Britain, for example, is entitled to her alimony. He also stressed that if the husband does not want his ex-wife to take his children away, he must provide a separate house for her in Qatar and continue paying alimony. This latter is often the case.

The position of divorced women in Qatari society, and whether they are allowed to remarry was also of interest. Most of my Qatari interviewees maintained that there exist no social taboos, and most definitely no religious ones, preventing women from contemplating and realizing a second marriage. The divorced woman, however, should observe a waiting period, *'iddah*, which is a probationary term that lasts for three months. This is to secure a child's legitimacy and identity should she be pregnant. If she is, then the waiting period lasts until the pregnancy is over and she has given birth. If the woman in question is not pregnant, then she may marry at the end of the waiting period. The chances for such a remarriage are high, but are mostly to a certain group of men – divorcés, widowers but rarely bachelors. The choice of a second marriage partner lies totally with the woman and she is allowed to represent herself at the ceremony. The dowry is sometimes less than what she obtained for her first marriage, although this may not necessarily be the case.

This does not mean all divorced women must remarry; some of them never do and continue to lead a normal life as there is no stigma attached to their position. The same cannot be said with regard to other Arab societies. Gulf countries in general have accepted the remarriage of women without creating an issue, most probably because this coincides with religious teachings which encourage marriage and greatly discourage celibacy.

No statistics on the question of divorce are available as yet, but, faced with problems in the midst of broad social and economic changes, one can understand the reasons for an increase in divorce rates as based on the verbal opinions of older Qatari women. These social transformations have also brought changes in women's status. With more education and work opportunities, women become less dependent on the husband and this gives them the opportunity of asking for a divorce without being afraid of their financial future. But this alleged increase in divorce rates cannot be attributed to women. An old Qatari woman believes that because it is easier for a young man to find a wife with whom he is acquainted before marriage, it is easier for him to divorce. This is an extremely prejudiced viewpoint, since reasons for divorce cannot be explained so lightly. We must also keep in mind that nowadays young men and women enjoy the benefits of social change, and the corresponding freedom in the choice of a marriage partner. They are more realistic in their views of freedom and social limitations. Divorce rates thus may be liable to diminish at this stage, when movement towards extensive change is slow, in order to avoid the inevitable uncertainties and their damaging effects on the Qatari family.

CHAPTER FOUR

The Role of Qatari Women within the Family

The Qatari woman's role in the private domain has been greatly influenced by the same economic factors that reshaped her life in the public sphere. There can be little doubt that social and economic changes have produced a definite impact on the structure, function and distribution of authority within the family unit, which in turn is reflected in women's status.

The impact of social change on the family unit

> *Hissa, her mother-in-law and other women sat in the kitchen waiting for their menfolk to finish the meal they had just prepared. When her husband, sons and other male relatives finished eating, the men left for the* majlis, *where they would sit down to welcome friends and neighbours, discuss everyday problems and lend a helping hand to anyone needing it. Hissa and the other women then sat down to eat before resuming their household chores.*

This fictional family, which was generally representative of society four decades ago, no longer exists. Yet such an image of a Qatari woman's family life is what persists in the minds of most Westerners, even among some living in Qatar. Even though such a scene isn't part of everyday life now, the fictional description of the home life of Qatari women is useful when assessing the changes that have occurred within the extended family, where in the past the mother-in-law had her own privileged sphere of influence over other female members of the family, where seclusion was still highly valued and adhered to, and where society, neighbourhood and family solidarity were part of everyday life. But if we are assuming that this image has changed, in which direction is the change heading and what instigated it?

The extended family of the pre-oil era was not only a social necessity (a continuation of the tribal system), but also an economic one, where members of the same family, living in a society of scarce resources, had to collaborate in the production process to achieve better, more worthwhile results. Usually, the head of the family owned the production means, the pearling or commercial ships, and he employed almost all the members of his extended family to work collectively in pearling, shipbuilding or whatever. Women and children also formed an integral part of the production process. Qatari children were taught professions, and when they reached a certain age (thirteen upwards) became actively involved in the family business. The extended family provided individual members with much-needed economic and social security. In order to preserve the internal unity and economic status of the extended family, intermarriage between its members was practically essential. The head of the family assigned duties, distributed profits and reconciled any conflicting parties.

The economic contribution of women (as described in detail in Chapter 1), was either within the family unit or, if the extra income was required, outside it. We have already mentioned the fact that women enjoyed more decision-making power than they appeared to. This was not the obvious practice because of certain customs and traditions that were strictly followed at the time. The fictional situation described above can be explained by the fact that strangers were usually invited to eat with male family members, but women could not join in. In addition, the limited resources at the time meant that for lunch, for instance, they could afford to cook only one big meal. And according to Arab traditions of hospitality the whole meal would be offered to the guests whilst women did not keep food aside for themselves.

Change occurred when Qatar began reaping the profits of oil revenues, and the government assumed the role of family head providing the individual with social, judicial and economic security. The provisions of the Fundamental Constitution of Qatar, Article 7 illustrate the importance attached to the family, stressing that:

> *The family is the base of society. It is supported by religion, morals and love of the country. The law shall regulate the methods which ensure its protection from all weaknesses, enforcing its structure, strengthening its ties, and pay special attention to motherhood and children.*

Various laws were passed to protect the weaker individual members of the family (divorcées, widows and orphans), and educated women were able to enter the field of paid work. The social welfare state provided the individual with the same care and security enjoyed under the extended family unit of pearling days. With more affluence and the ensuing greater security outside the extended family, people could afford to live in separate houses of their own, a trend further encouraged through government housing schemes, which naturally provided for nuclear family units.

In addition to structural changes, the distribution and exercise of authority within the family was subject to change; economic independence freed the individual from the various dictates of older family members (father, uncles etc.), and thus decision-making became a more personal affair, whether with regard to major issues like the choice of marriage partner, for example, or less important questions such as way of dress, choice of friends, etc. The younger generation within the new family set-up has come to reject more and more what they call the interference of the older generation in their private affairs. Owing to the presence of more lenient mediators in the parents, these clashes between two opposed mentalities have not become a serious social issue. The differences of opinion between the first and third generations – grandparents and grandchildren respectively – are quite normal; and while the second generation (parents) has been able to reconcile old and new, having witnessed and lived through the important changes during the last twenty years, the third generation has difficulty in understanding certain old customs which seem meaningless at this particular stage of social change.

This is strongly evident in what Amina, a young Qatari woman, told me regarding this issue: "We used to live with my grandfather and grandmother, but everybody interfered in our way of life, and even if my parents agreed on something, the rest of the family strongly opposed it. I wanted to study in a mixed school, my parents agreed, but the older people in the family were completely against it. Now that we live in a separate house, it's much better for us; of course, we still visit our grandparents and the rest of the family quite often, but we don't live together anymore. You see, now I can travel abroad ... I've been to London and Paris all on my own, my parents didn't object because they trust me."

In the nuclear family, therefore, a person enjoys more freedom because a smaller number of people are involved in the process of decision-making.

Recent studies by Professor Johaina Al Issa (1975) and Levon Melikian (1976–8), relying on the sample method, revealed that out of 86 Qatari families 36 lived on their own, 15 with the wife's parents, 20 with the husband's and 15 with both families. Thus, 42 per cent of the sample are nuclear families while 58 per cent belong to an extended family unit.

At the 1981 seminar, held in Abu Dhabi, examining the influences of oil wealth in promoting social change, the Qatari sociologist Professor Johaina Al Issa concluded that until forty years ago, the extended family unit was prevalent, but that changes brought about by affluence, education and changing values have led to a shift in structure, function and distribution of authority, thereby giving birth to a more independent nuclear unit. Professor Johaina relied on statistical studies (1975), which revealed that the size of the average family was between six and eight members. In addition to this, she points out that individuals have also changed their ideas on the ideal number of children a couple should have; a census carried out among male and female students at Qatar University yielded the view that either four or five children were ideal.

These changing values have made a strong impact on the surrounding neighbourhood which formerly represented an extension of the family unit. *Al fareej*, or the neighbourhood, was where communal solidarity and cooperation were vital for survival. The process of collective production, which preserved the extended family, also created strong amicable relations between residents of the same area, and created a neighbourhood identity. *Al mufazaa*, or helping each other without expecting any financial or material reward, was one aspect of such solidarity; men would help each other in building houses, digging wells or making traps to catch fish (*masaker*). Strong collaboration, therefore, was not only limited to tribal relations within the extended family, but embraced cordial and affable behaviour towards one's neighbours, a practice which is gradually waning. Nowadays, as many of my interviewees pointed out, everyone is busy working hard during the day, so it is only natural that sometimes neighbours hardly know each other. If an individual ever finds himself in the position where he requires material assistance, he can always turn to the government for help rather than ask his neighbour.

In Gulf societies, the challenges facing the family unit are of a different nature from those faced by Western societies. In the long term, they might head in the same direction once they become subject to the same forces. For instance, in the USA, experts argue that rising divorce rates, declining marriage and fertility rates, and rising numbers of women leaving home for paid work are basic threats to the family. This analysis of the effect economic and political change exert on the extended family of assorted relatives, all living under the same roof, cannot really be complete unless it is related to the subsequent transformation of the woman's role within her family.

Women in the home

In the past, the ceremonial transfer of the bride to her parents-in-law's house symbolized the transfer of a young girl enjoying a carefree existence into a different role, where she became subject to many social pressures and duties. On the other hand, once a bride, the Qatari woman also became entitled to certain financial and moral rights as she moved into the more prestigious status of wedded wife.

In a previous chapter we explored the traditional form of marriage, where the groom's mother played a major role in the choice of a bride for her son, and where the married couple ultimately lived with the groom's family, the "balance of power" lying in the hands of older members of the extended family. Sociologists have argued that within every family there exists a multiple structure whereby instrumental power – dealing mainly with the external system – lies with male members (father/husband), while the expressive power, which deals exclusively with the internal system, is exercised by the female members of the family. This has certainly been the case in Qatar, the groom's parents making practically all the important decisions. But with the ever-increasing shift towards independent nuclear entities, there has been a transfer of power to bride and groom. Advice and guidance are still acceptable from parents-in-law, and these represent the final vestige of the authority they once exerted over the married couple. The expressive power, therefore, has changed hands from the mother-in-law to the wife, and it will become clear that, as a result of the social transformations undergone by Qataris in education, work and travelling, women now also enjoy part of the instrumental power of men.

In the past, and even nowadays, where the newly-married couple share the same house as the extended family, the mother-in-law was the person responsible for assigning duties to be carried out by all the female members of the household. Those newly-weds who still choose to live within the extended family system now prefer to have their own separate quarters which, naturally, assure them a greater degree of independence from older members. Many of my informants stressed how the mother waited anxiously for her son to marry, as this meant "a daughter-in-law to assist her with household chores, and grandchildren to bring joy and happiness to her life". These were definitely the basic spheres where her influence manifested itself.

Housework was tiring and varied, and only the rich (a minority in the past) could afford to keep servants. The rest divided the many difficult chores amongst themselves, and the newly-married bride had her fair share of work even if there were other women in the house. Unlike most of today's wives, who are able to enjoy the many benefits of modernization and affluence which facilitate household chores, in the old days a bride's lot was not a happy one, though she would rarely complain as there was relatively little even her husband could do to remedy the unhappy situation.

In Arab tradition, respect for one's elders was of paramount importance, and the newly-married couple would strictly abide by any set of rules imposed by their parents. Even nowadays, this respect continues as it stems from the religious aspect of the parent/child relationship, based on mutual obligations and reciprocal arrangements. Because parents may sometimes become physically weak, impatient, hypersensitive and perhaps suffer from misjudgements occasionally, abuses of parental authority might occur. Basic provisions were made in Islam to govern the individual's relationship with his parents. *Ihsan* is the root of such close ties, and this means showing kindness, compassion, charity and reverence towards one's parents. The mother is also the subject of many Koranic verses and prophetic traditions which attach a great deal of love and respect to her. The Prophet Mohammed is reported to have answered a son inquiring which parent to cherish more, by saying "Your mother" three times, and the fourth time "Your father". Many Qatari proverbs also underline the importance attached to the mother: "Lucky is the man who has a mother at home", "I love you my (maternal) uncle for in you is the smell of my mother."

Respect for one's parents is a unifying force in Arab societies. Nowadays, the younger members of a Qatari family no longer depend to a great extent on the protection and support provided by the older members of their family. Yet the father's house is still open to receive happily at any time the members of his family, and some fathers still provide for their sons and daughters in the form of regular gifts and material support.

Moral support or guidance was also provided for the newly-married couple. The mother-in-law, in this respect, played the role of a real mother for the bride who, during the first few years of marriage, would invariably be going through adolescence. Having herself lived through the same experience, the mother-in-law provided much-needed advice on marital as well as everyday affairs. Such counsel is hardly required nowadays because of the rising marriage age and the effect of mass media. Marital issues are now regularly discussed in newspapers and women's magazines, and the subject is also treated on radio and television in the shape of well-documented plays and serials. Even in religious programmes, the problems of marriage are profoundly discussed. Today's bride faces very different obstacles to her counterpart of forty years ago, especially if she is a working woman. We shall be dealing with these problems in the final chapter.

The mother-in-law/daughter-in-law relationship, therefore, has changed from the daughter-in-law's complete resignation to and acceptance of her mother-in-law's overwhelming authority, to a much less one-sided one, where self-assertion on the daughter-in-law's side is more evident. This is certainly true with regard to the educated, more affluent couples living away from the extended family. Nevertheless, it is understandably difficult for the mother-in-law to abandon readily her age-old influential status, so we find that whenever possible she still exerts some influence, though far more indirectly than before.

Children's upbringing

The mother-in-law usually voiced the family's desire for grandchildren, whose number was neither limited nor planned. This trend persisted for many reasons: the high mortality rate due to the lack of health services, the low cost of having and rearing children, and fatalistic beliefs (God provides for every child, etc.). Early marriage also affected birth rates, since it made possible a longer reproductive life, as did the tribal nature of society where large families were a source of pride. Big families are considered reputable not just because of their wealth and influence, but also because of their large number. That is why quantitative factors are as important as qualitative attributes.

This concept still exists in certain Arab societies, where quantitative factors are as important as qualitative ones. It is also widely believed that a high birth rate is more of an Islamic tradition than an enforced religious practice, especially as Islam is not opposed in principle to family planning. In fact Islamic law seems to urge the use of individual voluntary measures to space out the children or regulate the family size for health or economic reasons. The Holy Koran extends the lactation/nursing period to two years, and the Prophet warned against the suckling of a child by its pregnant mother. This implies that some form of contraception should be used. This argument is by no means unanimously adopted by Muslim scholars, but it is slowly gaining momentum. In

Qatar we find that birth control is not really a Government concern as overpopulation has never been a pressing problem in Gulf societies. Quite the contrary, larger-sized families are actually encouraged in order to increase the number of nationals and ensure a future Qatari work force, instead of imported foreign labour. The Government provides for free education and health services, and many other benefits that now make child rearing a shared responsibility. Nevertheless, following several visits to the women's hospital, it was evident that contraceptives are provided for and used by Qatari women who want to space out their children. It should be clear that those who resort to family planning are the new generation of women who can benefit from Government facilities, and are well aware of the physical as well as social need to plan their families.

Thirty years ago, this unawareness of the religious permissibility of family planning usually led to consecutive pregnancies and I still recall how an old Qatari woman described the difficulties of bringing up children in the past, by saying, "We usually had a baby on our lap and another in our tummy." Abortion is a different, far more complex issue and is not accepted as a form of family planning unless it is practised to save an endangered mother's life.

Having a baby was and to a great extent still is a crucial testing-ground for any wife, where failure to conceive meant that the husband could practise his religious right to remarry. The groom's mother would encourage her son to take a second wife who could bear his children. Complete success was achieved when the wife gave birth to a baby boy first, a male who carried the family name. This is still generally true of Qataris and Arabs from all walks of life. A related popular saying which means success and achievement is *"Jabat walad"*, or "She gave birth to a boy". Nevertheless, girls were not frowned upon even though they were considered a moral burden, because of the views concerning chastity and honour. The Prophet Mohammed welcomed baby girls in his famous *Hadith* saying,

> *"He who had a daughter and disciplined her well and educated her as best he could, this daughter would be his shield from Hell."*

A song from Qatari folklore reflects the preference for baby boys, and the welcoming of baby girls afterwards:

> *"I ask our Compassionate God,*
> *To grant Sharifa a baby boy*
> *And follow it with a baby girl."*

At any rate, girls are better received nowadays by all family members, especially as they are no longer a financal burden, less of a moral burden and the recipients of many financial benefits when married.

The birth of a child was usually accompanied by certain rituals and local customs. In the old days, the expectant mother would go to her parents' house to have the baby, with the help of a midwife. Of course, nowadays, the hospital provides for such close care and attention, but many mothers still wish to be with their daughters at the moment of childbirth. The sex of the newly-born was not immediately revealed for fear of the evil eye if it were a boy, and in order not to disappoint the mother if it were a girl. Sprinkling some salt under the baby's pillow to ward off evil spirits was also a common superstitious practice. These customs are rapidly disappearing now that the majority of women have their babies in hospital, and the person bearing the good news announcing a baby boy to the waiting father is generously rewarded. One of the traditions still adhered to is putting *kohl* on the eyes of a new-born child, for medicinal and aesthetic purposes. One custom that has religious roots is reciting the Muslim call to prayer in the baby's ears (carried out by the father), so that the first thing it may hear is the name of Allah, and hence grow up to be a good Muslim.

Certain celebrations invariably followed a birth, and within the first few days of delivery, singing and banging of drums took place outside the baby's house where relatives and neighbours could share in the joy of the occasion. On the seventh day following the birth, a special breakfast was prepared by the family to which neighbours and family members were invited; the baby was bathed and some people would put a gold ring in his bath water in the hope he would grow up to be rich and lucky. This particular custom has vanished almost completely, as beliefs have changed and a child's future is definitely more secure than in the days of pearling. On the fortieth day following the birth, a more important celebration still takes place where sheep are slaughtered in the name of the baby, and distributed to the poor and needy. This *al tamimah* is an old Islamic tradition.

The actual process of bringing up a child was mainly the responsibility of the wife's mother-in-law when the married couple lived with the husband's family, as was mostly the case, or of the wife's mother if they remained with her parents. Children love and cherish their grandmother, whom they address as *umi al o'da*, "my older mother". The grandmother's role was very important as she exercised all the expressive power within the family, and bringing up her grandchildren the way she saw fit was an extension of this authority, strengthened by her presence in the house. Naturally, this does not imply that the grandmother did not love her grandchildren, but rather it explains why she dedicated so much time and effort to their correct upbringing. In cases where the grandmother's help and guidance is still required, her influence remains great in the early formative years, but as children grow up her hold wanes, though never their love and respect for her.

Boys and girls normally played together in the same *fareej* until they were ten or twelve years old. Once this stage of growing up was reached, boys were taken under the father's wing, as they belonged to the male world and were entitled to all its privileges. The boy accompanied his father to the mosque, attended male gatherings in the *majlis*, and in addition to his Koranic education (or regular schooling later on) was introduced to his father's profession. A most important aspect of his belonging to the world of men was the boy's feeling of superiority over his sisters and sometimes even over his mother. This is currently undergoing change, and these superior attitudes are being toned down by education and women's new opportunities for working outside the home.

Girls, on the other hand, remained in female circles where they were taught to recite the Koran, pray, and carry out some of the minor household chores. This is also changing according to Mr Naser Al 'Othman, who explains: "Compared to the past, there's a great deal of mixing now within the family circle." Nevertheless, women still enjoy their own exclusive gatherings, where men are not allowed. Obviously, sexual roles are still deeply engraved in children; girls play with dolls and are conditioned to learning women's work, while boys occupy themselves with traditionally more masculine roles and functions. This is essential to maintain the fabric of every society, and even in the West arguments between advocates and opponents of the sexual role still rage unabated.

The husband/wife relationship

Privacy, in the real sense of the word, hardly existed in the home of the extended family. The actual construction of old houses, where all the rooms were adjacent to one another with a courtyard in the middle, was hardly conducive to secrecy, and thus practically every little detail of the newly-married couple's lives was common knowledge to the rest of the family who, through curiosity, would scrutinize most of their actions. Moreover, the family normally shared the same reception areas for men and women, which meant that there was very little time the new husband and wife could actually spend alone together. This made life quite difficult by our own modern standards of judgement, as it necessarily imposed a code of conduct on both husband and wife, one which was perhaps alien to their characters. The husband, for example, had to behave according to a certain set of traditions whereby he had to prove that he was man of the house. To help his wife in everyday household chores was positively unthinkable and he would thereby taint his masculine image, being discouraged from doing so by his parents anyway. The wife was also faced with the mammoth task of being up to the parents-in-law's expectations, as well as her husband's.

Where the husband and wife live in a house of their own, the situation is radically different, and their relationship can be allowed to flourish. However, some might argue that the change is for the worse, as the presence of other family members can sometimes act as a deterrent to moments of extreme anger or disagreement, encouraging rapid reconciliation. This, however, would appear to be a very superficial argument, as most young Qataris would stress that the basic root of the problem will remain unsolved, and once the seeds of discontent are sown they can rapidly grow out of all proportion. Nevertheless, total privacy does not really exist in those wealthy nuclear-family homes where nannies and servants share the privacy.

With regard to the religious aspect, in marriage a

Qatari woman assumes a new marital status only as the wife of her husband but she retains her old lineal one. She is always referred to by her maiden name and never changes it. Thus her new marital rights in no way absorb or negate her former individual prerogatives or independent personality as far as private possessions and acquisitions are concerned. Neither the husband nor the wife acquires any "right" to the other's property by reason of marriage, although there do exist definite mutual rights in inheritance. Thus the wife is most certainly afforded a great deal of protection by society, being allowed to retain – in addition to her dowry, which includes jewellery etc. – any goods acquired through inheritance, by gift, or by the fruits of her own labour and investment. She is also allowed to hold property in her own name and dispose of it independently as she sees fit. In this respect, Koranic laws fifteen centuries ago gave women the sort of rights that Western women's liberation movements until only recently had to fight long and hard for. In the United States, for example, a wife had no legal control over her own property until the late nineteenth century, when women were given the right to negotiate contracts, run their own businesses and keep their own earnings.

In Belgium, a husband can choose to remain at home and still benefit from the social securities of his working wife. In this way, the Belgian woman has a legal duty to support her husband. The Muslim woman can do so through her own choice, but she may ask for and be granted a divorce if the husband is so poor that he cannot afford the expense of keeping her.

Apart from the husband's duty to provide support and economic security for his family, he is also commanded by the law of God to treat his wife with equity, to respect her feelings, and show kindness and consideration. She must not be treated with aversion or subjected to suspense and uncertainty. No man is allowed to keep his wife if he intends inflicting harm on her, or if he has no love or sympathy for her. If this is the case, she has the full right to be freed from the marital bond. The husband is also required to provide his wife with the help and service to which she was accustomed before marriage.

According to some jurists, the wife is under no legal obligation to carry out the daily routine housework, though she may do so and of course usually does. The Prophet and his companions set an example by helping their wives at home. Salaries for housewives was a point of discussion but only few of my male interviewees agreed with the idea. Most of them rejected it on the basis that it is degrading to give the wife a salary as if she were a servant. As one of them explained, "We don't give salaries ... but we buy almost anything the wife asks for, and give her the money she needs, within our financial abilities."

Most of my Western women interviewees resented the fact they had to do the shopping for the family and drive the children to and from school. Qatari women do not have the same chore as it has always been the tradition not to let women go to the market; it was considered unrespectable for a woman to do so. The market-place itself is not thought of highly by Arab social standards. Nowadays, however, more and more Qatari women go shopping with their husbands, and this provides an outlet from the routine of family life.

Driving a car is still very much a limited privilege for Qatari women, and only few working women are given a licence. For Western women living in Doha, this seemed significant when assessing how much freedom their Qatari counterparts really enjoy. It is true that being able to drive her own car gives a woman great freedom of movement, but it is also true that an older member of the family usually knows when and where a girl is going. The husband too is usually told beforehand and on no account would a woman go wherever she wished without telling the members of her family. Whether they are driving or a driver is taking them, a specific destination should be declared. When asked whether more Qatari women should be given driving licences, a good number of the male interviewees agreed, on condition that they actually worked. Mohammed 'Abdullah summed up their sentiments: "I don't see why women should not drive. There are some Qatari women who drive their own cars. They're working, of course. You see, forty years ago women were secluded from men. Doha was a small place, there were few streets, no cars ... it was very different ... but now women are educated, they work, and the need for them to drive is becoming more important." Most objections stem from fear of misuse of such freedom, while some complained on the basis that the car might break down or the woman might have an accident and find herself in an embarrassing situation. All opponents, however, were basically concerned for the women's welfare and respectability. Not all women are in favour of driving a car as most of them can afford a driver, but a sector of university girls was strongly in favour of driving cars themselves for reasons of convenience.

Another issue related to family life which seems representative of women's status was the fact that Qatari men do not escort their wives to mixed parties and social gatherings (i.e. occasions where people of different nationalities socialize together). Fahd Al Khater expressed his views on this subject: "It is difficult to take one's wife to such parties because of the language barrier. If she doesn't speak good English she will be embarrassed and reticent, and the husband cannot be interpreter all the time ... also, the foreign people who invited us would be embarrassed. But I know some Qatari husbands who take their wives; even if they don't speak English, most can understand." This attitude is quite typical of the young Qataris who, through their job or education, have often mingled with English-speaking people. Generally, the presence of strange men is not welcomed by most Qataris when accompanied by their wives because of the embarrassment which is closely linked to the traditional feeling of female honour.

Women's activities outside the home

In the past, women's activities outside the home were very limited and centred mainly on the social aspects of life. Apart from marriage and childbirth, there were also two major events for women's gatherings and celebrations in public. These occurred during the two Muslim feasts *'Eid al-Fitr* and *'Eid al-Adha*, and a comprehensive description of these will be provided in Chapter 5.

Social gatherings were and still are the nucleus of practically all activities. Women often visit each other in groups, and these gatherings normally take place in the afternoon following the *'asr* prayer. After exchanging greetings and inquiring about each family's well-being, coffee is passed round. A large tray bearing cakes, fruit and nuts is placed in front of the older women. However, when I went to a similar gathering, which is still very popular amongst the older generation of Qatari women, the tray was first placed before me. Frankincense or rose-water is then passed round. Tea is brought and usually more coffee is drunk before the occasion comes to an end.

These women's gatherings served more purpose than just entertainment. The guests could exchange information and delve into the secrets of the men's world. Through their various roles as intermediaries, older Qatari women knew a great deal about the privileged world of men, while men remained largely ignorant of the women's world. In such circles, older women looking for suitable brides for their sons were provided with the opportunity of finding a prospective partner, and collecting all the necessary information about whoever was nubile. This sometimes did not work out, as one young woman explained. When her mother was looking for a bride for her brother, she came to hear of a suitable girl at such a gathering who was described as exquisitely beautiful. Luckily, before the mother went officially to see and thus engage the girl to her son, she saw the girl herself at another gathering. The girl was not at all beautiful and possessed none of the traits attributed to her. In a sex-segregated society where young men and women were rarely allowed to mix, these gatherings served the important function of arranging marriages, apart from offering women the opportunity to help each other with the more difficult household chores. They also provided an emotional outlet where friends got together and openly discussed their problems. Gossip, a feature of many women's lives, was another aspect of such gatherings where women could sometimes make or break the image of other women or the reputation of eligible girls in society. Apart from these meetings, women used the enclosed balconies which projected from the outer walls of their houses and which had wooden screens in order to see what went on in the street without being seen.

Agents of change

In her book on women and modernization in North Yemen, *Changing Veils*, Carla Makhlouf defines as agents of change: "those institutions which constitute new bases of association and provide alternatives either in the form of social roles, or in the form of images and legitimizations to the familial roles and images to which women are traditionally confined." In Qatar, these agents of change have been the same as anywhere else: school, university, educational institutes, scholarship and work opportunities at various Ministries, etc. Yet there do exist other organizations whose aim is to effect changes in the older women who are not subject to the direct influence of the previously-mentioned institutions. These include adult and literacy programmes for women and the Vocational Training Centre. Both generations meet at the Qatari Women's Association, "The Women's Branch of the Qatar Red Crescent Society".

Adult education and literacy programmes for women
Sheikhah is a Qatari woman in her mid-thirties, married, with six children. She married at thirteen and never had the chance to pursue her education until her children grew up, and the Government provided for literacy and adult educational centres for women.

I met Sheikhah at the Red Crescent Society during the summer activities; she is full of ambition and desire to improve her status. "I must know what my children are talking about," she said. "I must understand and help them. You see, things have changed, and I'm not there just to cook, wash and clean. I must understand them so they can feel I'm their friend. Of course, they love and respect me, but they would even more if I were educated and had a degree. My father made me leave school to get married ..." Sheikhah quoted Koranic verses which underline her argument:

> *"Read, in the name of thy Lord and Cherisher,*
> *who created man out of a mere clot of congealed*
> *blood. Read! And thy Lord is most bountiful. He*
> *who taught the use of the pen, taught man that*
> *which he knew not."*
> SURA 96 1–2

"You see, God encourages all Muslims to learn, whether male or female, and many sayings of the Prophet (*Hadith*) stress this. Now we have a chance to catch up." Sheikhah has not reached the secondary stage of education, and wants to continue. "The opportunity is there. We go to evening classes and we can do all the household chores in the morning. Many other women have done the same. Of course, it gets more difficult when you are older, but life is easier now, and I can find time to study."

Not all women are so ambitious and some will not persevere. Obviously, women who join adult education classes should have had formal education up to primary level, but literacy programmes are for women who have had very little, if indeed any education at all. Adult education for men first began in the early fifties. Regular education in Qatar started at practically the same time, in the mid-fifties. It was much needed, and has played a great role in educating many Qataris at a crucial time in the development of their country. Literacy classes and adult education for women began in 1976, as decreed by the Council of Ministers. Statistics issued by the Ministry of Education revealed the number of applications when the programme was initiated to be 1319, and the figures have now increased to 2102. Originally, two evening centres were established, but, owing to increasing numbers of women enrolling, this rose to fifteen centres (some in schools assigned for the job) in 1980.

The literacy classes are divided into four stages, the final phase bringing primary education to an end, whilst adult education provides for preparatory and secondary levels. Certificates are awarded, and students are allowed to start their adult education once they have passed the fourth stage of the literacy programme. Curricula and examinations at the evening classes are the same as those of regular daytime schools. Qualified teachers are provided at all stages, having previously been trained for the difficult task of dealing with older students, and Arab experts on literacy curricula are frequently invited to advise on setting programmes. This way, literacy programmes for women are sure to include subjects that are related to women's health, moral and personal needs, as well as family affairs and children's upbringing. With full awareness of the vital part an educated mother plays in a developing society, the programme is designed not just to teach women how to read and write, but also to enlighten them and upgrade their social role.

In other fields, women's libraries have been established which all female students can use. Zobaidah Saleh is the librarian of the first such library, *"Al Khansa."* She explains: "The Qatari officials realize women's need for such a library and the difficulties in using the other libraries; they can't change society overnight, so they establish these women's libraries. We have all sorts of books and we can get anything from the main library, *'Dar Al Kutub'."*

It could be argued that this will further encourage the segregation between the sexes, but what is happening in Britain and the United States makes us wonder. In Britain there is a suggestion to provide a special coach for women in the underground because of the rising rate of incidents of rape and harassment. In the US women's banks (already a trend in Saudi Arabia) are flourishing. The women's banks are the products of the same social pressures that have led to an array of measures in the US to improve the position of women. The same year the first such bank was opened, Congress passed the Equal Opportunities Act which made it illegal for banks to discriminate against women in making loans.

The Vocational Training Institute

This institute was established by the Ministry of Labour and Social Affairs in the knowledge that certain women such as widows and divorcées, who could benefit from the Ministry's Welfare Schemes, were not necessarily able to meet their own needs with their monthly cheque alone and hence should be afforded the possibility of learning some vocation in order to upgrade their financial position, and help them contribute to the process of development. The actual centre was established in 1975, but did not begin functioning properly until two years later. It accepts any Qatari woman whose education has attained the fifth primary grade and who is physically fit. No age limit has been imposed, other than that prospective candidates should be at least fifteen years old. Even though the institute's programmes are directed mainly at widows and divorcées, girls are also welcomed and trained in the same manner.

Mariam 'Ali Al Khalaf is a social supervisor at the institute, and she expressed great enthusiasm about the training programmes they offer. "Here, we can do something to help those women who find supporting a family alone a very difficult task. They all want to learn, and we've given them many choices in our various sections, which teach them sewing, home economics, handicrafts and embroidery, child care and first aid. The women attend daily from 7.30 a.m. until 11.00 a.m. The actual studying is practical rather than theoretical. It lasts for two years at the end of which the woman is given a diploma. They are paid for what they do, in addition to whatever social benefits they are entitled to, and transportation to and from the vocational centre is provided."

Plans are also being made to help the illiterate women who cannot join at the moment: "We are aiming to establish a section for the purpose of preserving traditional embroidery (*naqda* and *kurar*), and in this section we would be able to welcome this sector of Qatari women, train them and give them a chance to work. The Ministry is also considering the idea of opening a Government workshop which could employ the graduates from this centre, and could later produce enough products to cover local needs. For the time being, at the end of every year we have an exhibition of the work done by students, and later on the products are sent to the co-operative markets for sale."

Fatimah 'Abdullah is a middle-aged woman I met at the institute. She is very much in favour of vocational training: "If they don't give us this opportunity, we'll never have a chance to work. Mind you, some women prefer to live on their social welfare allowances rather than working ... they are lazy, it is wrong for them and for their country. In the past women worked hard, life was tough and difficult, but now despite the change, or maybe because of it, who knows, some don't want to do any kind of work. Even in the house they have the houseboy and cook, and they waste their time doing nothing, only visiting and going to the *souq* ... But this institute gives women who want to do something a chance to work."

Fatimah is widowed and is responsible for bringing up five children. She receives a monthly allowance under the social welfare scheme, yet she says: "Of course they increase our allowances ... the Government is very good ... it takes care of us, but why shouldn't we take care of ourselves and eventually relieve the Government of its burden. For me, I was always scared before I joined the institute, that the money might not be enough, something could happen and then I could do nothing to help my children. Now, I am more secure ... I know I can work and will continue to do so."

Some women do not share Fatimah's ideas, and

others who do are not physically capable of working. But the solution to the problem of whether to live on social security only, or work, has been solved by the Government. Monthly allowances continue until the woman is officially employed. We must also remember the influence of old traditions and customs encouraging women not to work, since by tradition they should not have to, and these are still deeply rooted in the age group of women who receive Government aid.

The Qatari Women's Association

For many years, enlightened Qatari women dreamt of having their own association which could be a symbol of their improved status in society, and which they hoped would eventually effect some change in other women, making them of useful service to society as a whole. This notion was positively encouraged by Qatari men on different occasions, mainly in newspaper articles. I've chosen to mention two articles reflecting such support. The first was written by Naser Al 'Othman, published in *Al Rayyah* newspaper under the headline "Where are the women's associations?". In a clear, intelligent style, he stresses that women constitute half of every society, and that they should correspondingly enjoy definite religious rights intended to preserve their integrity and freedom. He adds,

> *This talk is what we repeat in the* majlis, *offices and everywhere. But if we examine the actual facts of life, we find that it has rarely been put into common practice. Our society needs the woman's sincere efforts and abilities. I'm not asking women to throw away their Islamic veil, or mingle freely with men, or imitate men. No, they can do a great deal for their society without resorting to such extremes. We miss the presence of 'women's associations', run by*

women, which can be of benefit to society, and
give women the chance to make the most of their
free time, so often wasted in gossip.

Mr Al 'Othman concludes by mentioning the success of such associations in other Gulf countries.

Similarly, another article by Khalid Al Hajiri, also published in *Al Rayyah*, on March 1st 1981, said:

The content and target of such an association
should be clear, and the establishing of a
women's association should follow relevant
studies of other neighbouring associations,
whereby a proper evaluation can provide us with
suitable alternatives for our own society. The
association I speak of should have certain traits
that make it respond and react to society's needs
and the developing role of women. It is not meant
to be a place where women can compete in the
latest fashions, etc.

Mr Al Hajiri continues by saying that

... our society is a mixture of bedu *and* hadar
(city dwellers), poor and rich, the educated and
the illiterate, locals and foreigners. Yet women
everywhere have the same problems, and this
association should be the melting-pot of all such
groups, as well as a suitable meeting-ground. The
responsibility for establishing this association is
that of the enlightened and educated sector of our
women, who should make a concerted effort,
instead of just voicing their desire in newspapers.
It is equally our duty as husbands, fathers and
brothers to encourage our womenfolk and explain
to them the need for such voluntary work.

The first women's association in Qatar was created on the 22nd February 1982, with the full moral and financial support of the Government. It is known as "The Women's Branch of the Qatar Red Crescent Society". It has been provided with a well-furnished two-storey villa and supplied with the basic needs for its various activities. In her early thirties, Mariam Darwish is head of the branch, and when I asked her why a woman's association should be affiliated to the Red Crescent Society, she said: "The name is not important. We function as any other women's association, in addition to our duties as a branch of the Red Crescent Society. Our basic aim is to enlighten women and upgrade their status. We want to reach all sectors of Qatari women, all age groups and levels of education, from university professors to the simple woman. This way, women will use their spare time to carry out much-needed social services and upgrade their cultural, social and health standards and awareness. In order to achieve this, we've established committees to deal with these varied activities. We have the vocational training committee, social services committee, health committee, and the public relations, culture and information committee."

The Qatari Women's Association has been able to learn from its sister associations in the Gulf area, and has chosen the best, most rewarding activities, housing them all under one association. Asked if women's responses had been largely favourable, Mariam replied, "So far we have not encountered many problems ... our main problem has been women's cautious attitudes, actually taking the first step ... this is because they are no longer used to doing voluntary work. I am sure that, in time, larger numbers of women in Qatar (whether Qatari or not) will welcome participation in the social field ... they are naturally apprehensive of the first step, and that is why it has taken the woman so long to shoulder her social responsibilities."

The objectives and message of this association are encouraging. The women involved are very enthusiastic, and eager to prove to their menfolk that the chance they have been waiting for is well-earned. Mariam herself is a bright example of today's Qatari woman. She married young, but continued her education up to university level once her children had grown up. Mariam found a job at the university and enjoyed working there; she still does so in addition to her voluntary responsibilities at the women's association. Her ambitions were quite evident when I met her during the course of the radio interviews for my programme in 1980. She then voiced the need for a Qatari women's association, and the strong necessity to give women their rights within the framework of Islam. The next time I saw Mariam was two months after the formal opening of the association she had proposed.

During my frequent visits to the Red Crescent Society, I met many of Mariam's colleagues as well as women attending the association's activities and this enabled me to draw a realistic picture of the effort put into the women's association. Najah Nou'eimi is Deputy Head of the association, works at the university and is unmarried. I met her eight months after the society's inauguration, and I first wanted to know whether she thought they had achieved their aim of attracting greater numbers of participants. Najah told me that the numbers had increased, and that most women were encouraged to attend by their menfolk, who in turn went to the trouble of driving them to and from the premises. "Husbands and parents trust us, and know that it is far better for their womenfolk to come here and do or learn something rather than stay at home. Our committees provide for various activities ... on the vocational level, we provide typing courses in Arabic and soon, hopefully, in English, so that women can enter the field of work with additional or even basic vocational experience.

"Our social services committee organizes visits to

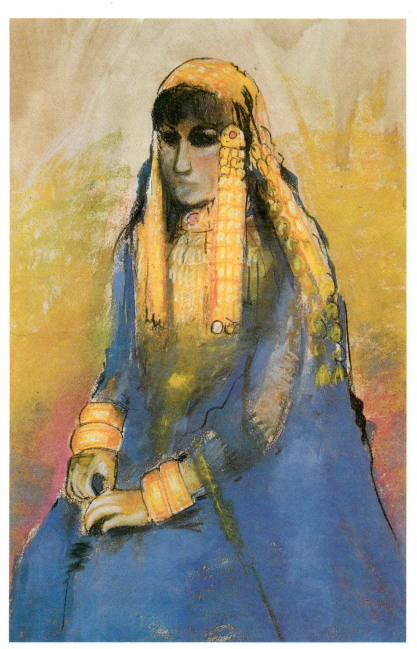

A Qatari bride wearing traditional gold jewellery

Top: Traditional gold bracelets (*banjari*)
Bottom left: *Al murtahish*, the "shiny" necklace
Bottom right: *Al ma'ra*

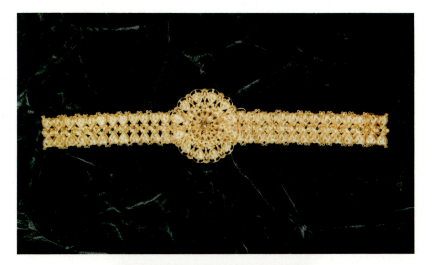

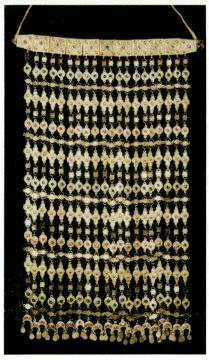

Top: *Al mehzam*, the embossed and enamelled gold belt
Bottom: *Al murta'ishah*, the "shaking" necklace

Top: *Al kaf*, the traditional wedding-day bracelet
   with attached rings
Bottom: Gold earrings, including (top left) *al shaghab*

Top: Two pairs of embroidered *sirwal* and some
gold buttons (*azirah*)
Bottom: The materials used for making *azirah*

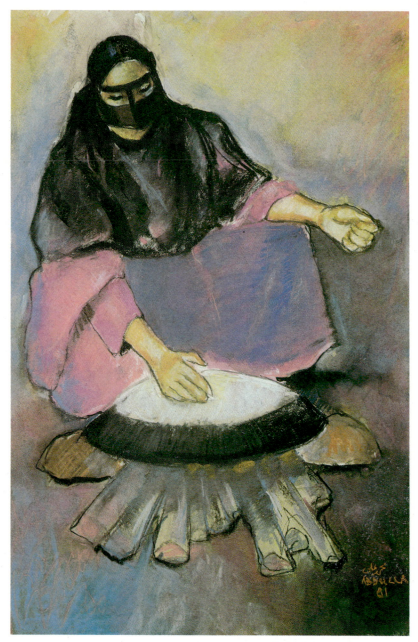

A Qatari woman making bread

A Qatari woman cooking

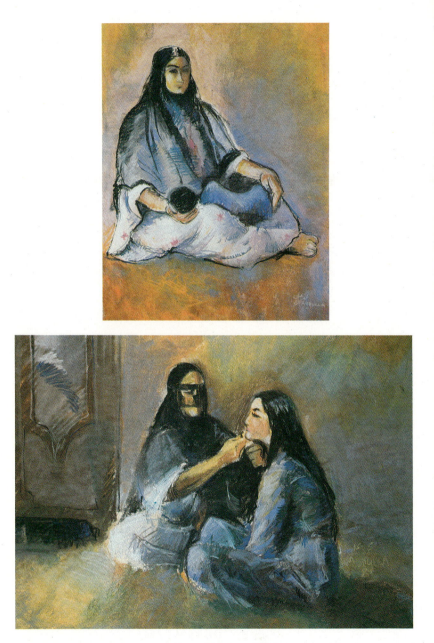

Top: A Qatari woman rocking a child
Bottom: A Qatari bride being prepared for her wedding

the elderly and to handicapped children in hospital.
Women distribute presents, and share feasts with
these people who need our love and attention. This
committee also studies some social problems and
public services, in collaboration with the Ministry of
Labour and Social Affairs, and that of Municipal
Affairs. During the summer, we've had the handicapped children's summer club, which aimed at
making the girls happy as well as providing them
with some vocational and educational abilities in
order to promote their psychological and social re-
habilitation. Our social committee also hopes to
expand its circle of activities to learn more about
distant villages in order to improve the standard of
living of their inhabitants. This committee has issued
what we expect to be a rather unusual edition of the
magazine *The Volunteer*, and will publish a monthly
booklet. Both are meant to inform women of our
functions and activities, and widen their scope of
knowledge."

The first edition of *The Volunteer* was well-planned,
covering a wide variety of topics ranging from the
latest discoveries in medicine, to short stories and
articles on Gulf affairs, written by the best Qatari
female writers and researchers. The Head of the
association wrote an article on the role of women in
Qatar, in which she touched on the bitter fighting in
Lebanon and the association's efforts to provide
badly-needed aid.

'Aisha 'Ali Mohammed is a librarian in the Humanities Department of Qatar University, and she
says: "The need for our activities is obvious, and we
started functioning effectively from the very start.
We've established contacts with the ladies in the
diplomatic corps, ambassadors' wives etc., in order to
organize regular meetings where each country could
exhibit its costumes, foods and cultural traditions.
This would give Qatari women a better chance to

become more acquainted with women from different nationalities and backgrounds." Najah Nou'eimi here stressed a point which seemed to be of great relevance: groups of Western women who wanted a closer view of Qatari women were welcome to visit the association at any time.

The culture and information committee organizes cultural evenings and lectures, which are attended by large numbers of women as they are basically public functions. This committee is headed by Mariam Al Saad, a well-known writer and journalist, and the committee itself helps in issuing the monthly bulletin and annual magazine. The health committee, too, provides lectures and information for members of the association as well as the general public; it also organizes visits to some houses with the aim of providing health guidance to mothers and house-wives.

The workshop committee provides sewing courses for women, in the hope of reviving this Qatari craft, and preserving it by teaching embroidery to women and girls in the association. During one of my visits, I met a lady who knew a great deal about embroidery, wanting to learn more on the subject and teach other women at the Red Crescent Society. Gamilah Ahmed Noor (mother of the Qatari artist Mohammed 'Ali 'Abdullah) is a very interesting person; she has seven children, and always wanted to do something constructive: "We didn't have servants, I used to do all my housework at night, washing and cleaning. It was not easy, and I would leave the cooking for the mornings. We cooked on the *sholah* (a gasoline stove), and I used to make time in the mornings to be able to do my embroidery and sewing."

Gamilah joined literacy classes and reached the second stage of preparatory. She originally wanted to go to the Vocational Training Institute to learn sewing and typing, "but it was in the mornings, and I have literacy classes in the evenings ... so I couldn't join, even though I wanted to so much. When this association was established, the impossible became feasible for me, and I came to learn typing and sewing. But when I saw the need for a woman who knew something about Qatar's heritage of embroidery, I offered my services. Of course, I had to drop my literacy evening classes, but I'm still studying at home and will sit the exam."

Gamilah's great interest in the Qatari heritage is shared by her son, Mohammed 'Ali, who is also a conscientious researcher in this field. She takes every opportunity to provide him with relevant information. She told me how, during one of her visits to Khor, a fishing town in the North, she had seen a bedouin woman, and seized the opportunity to discover how horse-saddles were woven. The bedouin took her to an old house and in one room showed her the weaving-machine attached to the ceiling. Although she arranged to buy it, when she returned the bedouin and weaving-machine had vanished.

Gamilah is in her early forties and doesn't wear the *batula*. Despite her inquisitive nature, she remains very humble: "I want to learn from others and benefit more ... I come here every day, and this gives me the chance to meet people and do something worthwhile."

The Qatari Women's Association is also studying the possibility of establishing a nursery under its supervision, and in collaboration with the Ministry of Health. A home for orphans is another project they are hoping to accomplish. They have a separate budget, face no financial problems, and the charity sales of their own products cover their immediate requirements.

Obviously, this association's functions and aspirations underline its usefulness in a developing society, where women can only be reached and taught by other women. Despite the claim that the association merely reflects the prejudice against women, it has most definitely functioned on the right basis. The women in charge are well aware of the sensitivities of their society, and carry out their duties accordingly: they express their views to the press and speak on radio, but will not allow their photographs to be printed. Quite understandably, they want to maintain a respectable image and their own credibility, away from public attention. Moreover, because the association is developing under the wing or protection of the Red Crescent Society, it has been able to attract increasing numbers of uneducated Qatari women. The many forms of activity provide various alternatives, and women go there to work rather than to socialize, which they can easily do at their own gatherings. In conclusion, it is a promising start for expansion into more active fields of social work for women in Qatar.

CHAPTER FIVE

Qatari Women's Ventures into the Arts and Literature

It is generally accepted that culture and art in all their manifestations are the product of man's interaction with his environment, history and religious convictions.

In the past, the Gulf's culture was closely related to the harsh climatic conditions, which forced its inhabitants to turn to the sea in search of a livelihood. As we have already observed in an earlier chapter, pearling and commerce constituted the basic economic realities of the area. Historically, Arabic culture was dominant, but Gulf societies were also subject to cultural infiltration from other alien communities such as India, East Africa and the Persian coast of the Arabian Gulf.

Qatar itself, a peninsula which stretches out into the Gulf waters like an open hand, was also subject to the same external influences, but nonetheless its art was distinguished by its emphasis on desert and sea. These are symbolic of the forces at work, the ever-changing, constant movement of waves lapping against the desert stillness and its traditions. This left a profound impression on practically all aspects of Qatar's cultural heritage. Literature and folklore were the product of stories based on the sea and diving life, and the verbal recitations of the nomads. In the arid desert with its monotonous landscape, the actual sound of the verse was of paramount importance to the bedouin, whose sense of poetry was therefore very acute. As a result of this, poetry was the literary genre of greatest merit to Arabs living in the desert, and became a complete form of expression in itself. In addition to this oral skill, there was also song, which accompanied an individual from birth until his death.

Oral arts were thus prevalent in the area, while visual arts assumed a secondary role. Religious objections to portraying living creatures were the basic reason for this. (Pictorial art, which is considered Western by some local Qatari artists, is an accompaniment of the oil era. It saw light in the fifties and its pioneers were Bahraini.) On a more practical level the colours available for painting were limited to two, blue (sea and sky) and yellow (desert). Because of this lack of variety, people in Qatar used to prefer bright, contrasting colours in order to alleviate visual boredom. For example, until ten or fifteen years ago, most houses were painted in strong, vivid hues, and women similarly wore brightly-coloured clothes.

The impact of the economic factor on the various art forms was also direct and decisive following the influence exerted by the oil boom. The new-found wealth led to the demolition of old houses where, in some cases, the full splendour of Arab architecture was most pronounced. Certain local crafts (embroidery, goldsmithing, weaving and dyeing of cloth and dhow building) have more or less disappeared, either because economically they are no longer viable, or else as a result of the replacement of traditional handiwork by machines and industry. Even in the

field of popular and folk songs, the new materialistic
way of life has left an important legacy, and stories
told by grandmothers along with children's songs
and lullabies of the past, especially *nabati* verses, are
now being collected by researchers in an effort to
revive them. This is especially understandable in a
multinational society, where a mixture of races and
cultures results in changes and alterations. Bearing
in mind also that many foreign nannies now look
after Qatari children, one can comprehend the ur-
gency behind such efforts.

The interest in preserving and documenting the
many aspects of Qatari folklore (including poetry,
songs and stories as well as crafts) is rapidly gaining
momentum in the private sphere, in addition to the
various Government departments' efforts in this field.
The Arab Gulf States' Folklore Centre was established
in 1981 with the aim of accomplishing this mission in
the whole Gulf area.

Researchers have already covered some aspects of
Qatari folklore – jewellery, *nabati* verse by male poets
and stories – but many other arts related to the
subject of this chapter, such as women's *nabati* verse,
embroidery, weaving and dyeing of cloth, are still
virgin territory for any researcher.

Weaving and dyeing

Qatari women were involved in textile weaving
and dyeing, which in their simpler forms were part of
every bedouin woman's life. Bedouin women used
sheep's and camel's wool to make the various cloths
for tents and rugs. The wool was spun by hand on a
wooden spindle called a *noul*. The wool was first
teased out of the fluffy mass and twisted as it
emerged, tied to a bobbin which acted both as a
weight to keep the fibres taut, and as a core on which
the thread would eventually be rolled. This was
obviously a slow procedure as women had to spin

different colours of wool separately.

Weaving these woollen threads was a laborious process. The loom employed was vertical, made of wood, with the warp threads hanging down, weighted, while the woman sat and passed the weft threads back and forth between the warp threads by hand, using a stick to beat the weft firmly into place. This was the only method known at the time. Tents were woven of different natural-coloured woollen threads in stripes (beige from camel and brown or white from sheep), but rugs and carpets were made from threads of contrasting colours, normally red or yellow, dyed by the women themselves. Herbs growing in the desert were used to dye these threads, and the designs were simple geometric ones, especially triangular shapes. Coloured cloth and dyes were only imported as late as the nineteenth century, when trade and commercial relations with India and East Africa increased considerably.

Embroidery

In the past, men and women wore a long simple dress with long sleeves, a *thaub*. The man's *thaub* was usually made of white cotton, the neckline and sleeves decorated with a simple form of embroidery known as *kurar*. This same type of embroidery was used on women's dresses, but had more intricate patterns and observed certain rules, whereby a red dress was embroidered with green and yellow, and a blue or black dress was embroidered with three different colours. These dresses were called *m'fahih*. *Abbas* for both men and women were embroidered with golden threads, and opened at the front. *Kurar* embroidery involved four women, each holding four threads in her hands. These threads were then plaited and resemble heavy chain stitch embroidery. These plaits were sewn vertically on to a dress or an *abba*, one plait next to the other and were either made with colourful silk threads, or silver and gold ones.

Golden threads (*zarri*) were mainly imported from India along with coloured silk threads (*braisim*), which were used for the various kinds of embroidery. There existed certain houses which were famous for their sewing and embroidery, and such renown was based on the houses' financial assets which enabled them to import gold and silver threads, silk and cloth from India, in addition to their skills in embroidery design.

Women also made small cotton caps for men, which they wore under the headcover. These caps, *gohfiahs*, were made of a piece of cotton, which was pierced with a palm-tree thorn so that women could sew between the holes. Later, when such caps became available in the market, this form of embroidery died out.

Embroidery on *sirwal*, or ladies' loose drawers, was introduced during the Umayyad dynasty to the Arab World, remaining very popular in this area, and this was enhanced by the importation of similar drawers from India. Many books on Gulf folklore which have illustrations of such *sirwal* only show those of Indian style, the embroidery being machine-done. Of course, these were also widely worn, but they do not truly represent the original embroidery patterns of the area. I was fortunate enough to obtain photographs of authentic Qatari embroidery forms.

Among the Qatari women I visited for the purpose of obtaining information about embroidery, were two ladies over sixty who embroidered women's dresses and *sirwal* or loose drawers. Moza and Bana Moham-med used the traditional forms of embroidery at one time in order to earn a living, and have continued to practise this art despite the fact they no longer have any financial need to do so. They embroider dresses and *sirwal* for themselves, relatives and friends as a hobby. Moza was extremely courteous and helpful and patiently explained everything, whilst demonstrating some of her skills, especially making buttons. She kept the simple tools of her trade in a bamboo basket and had a long wooden bobbin on which she could put different kinds and colours of thread. Moza pointed out that until sewing machines eventually became available, all the sewing had to be done by hand. Personally, she had never done any plain sewing, dedicating her talents to embroidery alone. The skill with which she made small golden buttons, *azirah*, fascinated me; she placed a small piece of cotton wool around a matchstick and continued rolling it until it took the shape of a small hollow ball. She then wrapped golden threads around it to make a beautiful kaftan-like button.

Bana Mohammad showed me some examples of *sirwal* embroidery and explained how each of the embroidery styles is carried out, and what each is named. The photographs I have taken (see colour section) clearly show the geometric patterns employed, which further underline their Islamic origin.

The stitch used on the *sirwal* in the photographs is satin stitch, where straight stitches are worked side by side. Each type of stitch had a different local name – for example, the triangular shaped embroidery on top of the straight horizontal lines of embroidery are known as *durus al khail* or "horse's teeth". Each straight line is known as *bikhiah*. Each design has its own name depending on the number of lines of *bikhiah* it has. The design on the orange *sirwal* is called *bu sitt* meaning that it has six lines.

The design in between these horizontal lines has its own name, the orange *sirwal* have diagonal lines of embroidery in golden, black or red threads. This is called *bu sitt lazz*; the chevron design (*dalaat*) on the other pair of *sirwal* is called *you ziyah*. The actual stitches are quite simple, but the difficulty lies in handling the golden threads which are rough and, unlike silk threads, not at all easy to use. This is why the embroiderer will normally sit on the floor and place the cloth being embroidered on her knee, having lined the area to be worked with another layer of material.

Once the work is finished, she presses a heavy object (*al misgal*) against the embroidery, which is placed on a wooden board. This gives the golden threads a better shape and texture and it also tones down the bright colours. This embroidery has now become a costly process, as each roll of thread costs about 40 riyals, whereas almost thirty years ago it could be bought for only one or two riyals. A pair of *sirwal* needed at least four or five rolls of gold thread.

In order to obtain a description of the *naqda* embroidery of the headcovers, *milfa'*, which are made of black gauze, I went to see Fatima, another older Qatari lady, in her late fifties. The embroidery is done with *khoos*, a kind of metallic straw, in silver or gold. No needle is required and this metal is inserted in and out of the small holes of the gauze to provide the shape needed. Usually, geometric patterns are employed in this kind of embroidery where no previous pattern is drawn. This *naqda* embroidery is not easy, and it takes women at least two weeks to finish one headcover, the standard length of which is two and a half metres. The *milfa'* was not embroidered or studded all over; at one end there were usually more intricate and elaborate designs called lace, while the rest was sparsely studded. The *milfa'* covered the head around the face, and the heavily embroidered area usually went across the chest.

Nowadays, few people still do this kind of embroidery, because the market has been taken over by India which exports these headcovers to the area at cheaper prices which local embroidery cannot match. Nevertheless a growing interest among the younger generations of Qatari women has led to a newer, more difficult kind of *naqda* embroidery being included on the whole piece of cloth. This kind of headcover is called a *shailah*, and is used mostly like a shawl and worn, heavily studded with silver, at wedding parties. This is also imported from India. *Naqda* embroidery was used to decorate women's dresses as well, but was given up when gold threads became available. Most probably they were easier to use and more designs could be employed.

Other forms of embroidery appeared when commerce with Basra and Bahrain became regular. These other kinds were widely used for decorating cushions in the *majlis*. Cushions constituted the basic furniture in the room where guests were received and were used instead of chairs. In this instance, leaf satin stitch, satin stitch and stem stitch were most common, though this is known as "school embroidery" (*khiyat al madrasa*). Usually, women would send a bedsheet or pillowcase to someone skilled in drawing, and she would come up with a design of either flowers or birds. The choice of colour scheme was left to the owner of the cloth. Naturally, this practice served the purpose of decorating the *majlis* in the best possible fashion with limited resources. Bedrooms were also decorated with embroidered bedsheets.

Nowadays, some of the embroidered clothes are either done locally in the old *souq* or else imported from India. Only a small group of old ladies still maintain the knowledge of and love for this type of work, while most of the new generation know very little about it.

Painting

The art of painting has only recently found a footing for itself in Qatari society. This was basically because of Islam's stand on pictorial art. It has sometimes been stated that the painting of a picture is forbidden in the Koran, but there is no specific mention of pictures in the Koran, and the only verse usually referred to in support of this condemnation is:

> *"Oh believers, wines and games of chance and*
> *statues and (divining) arrows are an*
> *abomination of Satan's handiwork; then avoid*
> *them."* SURA 5:90.

From this verse it is clear that the real object of the prohibition was the avoidance of idolatry which was prevalent before Islam. The theological basis for the condemnation of pictorial art can be found in the *Hadith* sayings of the Prophet. Yet the Prophet did not appear to have objected to the figures of men or animals on the woven stuffs with which his house in Medina was decorated, so long as they did not distract his attention when praying.

Architecture and calligraphy were the most important forms of Islamic artistic expression, an art which had a definite style, quite distinct from Christian art where diversity rather than uniformity was the characteristic. Thus architects worked out a scheme of building construction and decoration in harmony with the austerity and dignity of the faith. However, the art most highly valued was that of calligraphy, which had an important position because of its connection with the word of God. The calligrapher was usually engaged in copying the Koran.

In Qatar too the Islamic architectural influence has left a definite impact on the designs and decorative motifs of most buildings and houses. Big wooden engraved doors were works of art which are now either kept in the museum or revived in paintings. Painting itself has only recently been introduced to Qatar, and this form of art was taken up by Qatari artists less than two decades ago. Themes of such paintings ranged from local to Islamic as well as Arabic heritage. Exhibitions were held under the auspices of the Ministry of Education until 1972, when the State's full support and backing were given to Qatari artists. In 1980, the Qatari Fine Arts Society was formed with the purpose of promoting the works of art of its members and all Qatari artists, by setting up exhibitions and holding seminars. One of the members of this society is Wafika Sultan.

Wafika is a versatile Qatari lady artist who is one of the pioneers of modern art in Qatar. Born in 1952, she received her BA in Applied Art from Cairo University in 1974. Wafika has participated in all local exhibitions since 1972, the second Arab Artists' Federation exhibition in Rabat in 1976, Kuwait's fifth and sixth exhibitions of Arab artists, the Qatari Art Exhibition London-Paris in 1978, the Qatari Art Exhibition in Tunis in 1979, an exhibition of works of art in Morocco in 1979, and the first and second exhibitions of the Qatari Fine Arts Society in 1981 and 1982.

A determined woman, Wafika is an asset to Qatar Television where she works as controller of production affairs. Despite her varied administrative responsibilities and actual involvement in the production of television series, she still works as a set designer, because to her this is part of her real attachment to art. A mother and housewife, she finds little time to dedicate to her artistic skills. She strongly believes that the artist should be fully dedicated to art alone, but seems to realize the impracticality of this, saying, "Most of us, Qatari artists, have been given important posts where we have administrative responsibilities. This is because our country needs us here and at this stage. That is why it is impossible to sacrifice the services we render as government officials for the sake of art only. That doesn't mean that art is secondary in our lives ... it never was and never will be."

Wafika Sultan's style of painting reflects her pro-

fessional background as an artist. She makes use of
the different aspects of Qatari folklore to produce a
relevant form of art. Folk songs and proverbs are
usually used as titles to her paintings. The paintings
however are mostly symbolic, but have enough realism in them to make people perceive hidden mean-
ings. In one of her paintings, for example, she por-
trays an old wooden door and the decorative architectural motifs around it whilst the wall surrounding the
door is cracking and losing colour. This painting,
which she named *A Sample of Islamic Architecture*,
simply says that the beauty of the past (door and
motifs) is dying out with modern architectural
trends.

Wafika believes that the artist's role is to clarify,
intensify and interpret the world around him or her,
while at the same time sticking to his or her roots of
tradition. "This is where the 'realism' of the Qatari
artist manifests itself ... realism is what we have
dealt with since childhood when we made paintings
of reality or real life. Nowadays, some want to imitate
the West by resorting to surrealism while most artists
in Europe have gone back to realism."

Wafika believes that the Qatari artist must not
copy Western schools of painting which do not relate
to Arab societies. She says, "We should appreciate
them, know about them, but we must not follow them
and lose our character." That is why she feels more at
home with the works and styles of some Arab artists
like Salah Taher, Moukhtar or Yousif Francis. "They
speak a language I understand, and that is why I try
to speak the same language," she commented.

As far as sculpture is concerned, Wafika likes it
better but admits that this form of art is still
unacceptable to Qatari society at large. This is why
she displays her works of sculpture at home. She
stresses that artists must respect their society's
values, and in addition to this believes that sculpture

was not indigenous to Qatar because of the lack of basic materials like clay and wood which helped and enhanced sculpture's role in places like Africa or China. Also the presence in those countries of a variety of animals and of a rich natural environment helped a lot. In Qatar there is little of this varied nature.

Wafika is contemplating the idea of opening her own art gallery, which would show Qatari and Arab artists' works and aim at preserving Qatari folklore.

Amateur artists can use all the facilities available in the Free Art Workshop. A branch for women was opened in 1980, thus giving girls and women the chance to practise art as a hobby. This branch is open regularly to all Qatari as well as non-Qatari women interested in the arts. There is a young lady in charge of the women's section of the workshop, and her job is to provide the guidance and criticism needed to improve the standard of the amateurs. I joined this workshop while I was involved in writing the radio series, and stayed with it for six months, which enabled me to understand the way it functions. Most drawing materials are available and almost all of the girls and women who attend the workshop are interested in drawing or painting, rather than sculpture or pottery. Some married women are provided with the necessary materials to do their work at home. Newcomers use pencil first, and start with drawings of still life, moving on to colour work later. After a while they make sketches of local themes for a drawing. Sometimes short lectures on the history of art are given and slides of world-famous works of art are shown with necessary explanations.

Nevertheless, the workshop has not yet been able to achieve the purpose behind its conception, and that is to become the nucleus for cultural and artistic education, besides encouraging local talents. The building, which both women and men have to attend, is in a very inconvenient area, far away from most residential districts in Doha. There is thus a strong desire to move its location to make it more easily accessible. The special studies carried out with the intention of improving the status of the Free Art Workshop have resulted in the formation of a consultative committee comprising artists, representatives from the plastic arts, and officials from the Ministry of Education, in addition to people involved in culture and the arts in general. It has been agreed to provide the women's section of the workshop with two art teachers, and to pay those who excel. This project might help in developing the services of the Free Art Workshop from which Qatari women may benefit.

Badriyah Jassim is an amateur painter who was born in 1954. She now works as a lecturer in Home Economics at Qatar University. She is preparing for an MA in Dress Design. Badriyah's desire to draw started at a very young age, and she participated in various school exhibitions: a local exhibition in 1977, the fourth and fifth annual exhibitions of Qatari artists, and the first Qatari Fine Arts Society exhibition of 1981.

Badriyah concentrates on dress and jewellery, and draws them in great detail. This, she says, differentiates her work from other people's, especially as she dreams of becoming a dress designer for Gulf and Qatari women. Badriyah admits that she needs to study art, because she has the talent but needs guidance and practice to reshape her talent for professional standards.

Amina Kathem is another amateur painter who has been practising her talent since her school-days. She is now a lecturer in Sociology at Qatar University, and is preparing for an MA. Amina is an ambitious artist who seeks to improve her talent by reading books on art and frequenting the Free Art Workshop for guidance and advice. Amina took part in school exhibitions and participated in the Qatari Fine Arts

Society's exhibition in 1981 with a drawing in charcoal of a Qatari girl wearing traditional dress. Themes for her portraits are obviously derived from her environment, such as drawings of the games Qatari children used to play in the old days. Amina has the same inclination as Badriyah towards concentrating on women's clothes and jewellery, but she too, as yet, lacks the professional knowledge needed to improve the quality of her production.

The works of both artists were exhibited in 1981 by the Qatari Fine Arts Society, and were discussed during the seminar which followed. Some artists criticized the idea of putting amateur works alongside those of the more established artists, but the consensus of opinion was that these amateur artists should be encouraged by the Society and allowed to take part in such exhibitions, until they have established themselves, as inevitably only those who excel will persist and advance.

Singing

The rich Qatari heritage of folk songs reflect the joys and sorrows, traditions and customs of its people, and through it one can see what life in the past was like. Work songs were most popular, especially those related to the sea, the centre of economic activity, and pearl diving songs were numerous and varied in rhythm. Each of these songs accompanied a different activity of the pearling trip; spreading the sails, diving, rowing the ships, returning safely, etc. Because collective singing was an integral part of the pearling trip, each ship had to have *al naham*, the ship's singer, whose role was to encourage work on the ship during the day and entertain the exhausted crew when they were resting. Women were not involved in this form of singing, except when the returning pearling ships were sighted. Then they gathered on the seashore, singing and clapping. In their songs they begged the sea to bring their men safely to shore, and described the hardships of the pearling trips. This form of singing vanished when the pearling stopped.

Women had their own work-songs such as wheat-grinding songs, and these were sung by a group of women who used to gather to help each other in the tedious task of grinding. They used *al raha* as a grindstone. This consisted of two round pieces of stone, the upper one had a hole in which the wheat was put and a wooden handle to turn it round on top of the lower stone. Some songs were of general themes, while others described the wheat-grinding process and the qualities of *al raha*. The same can be said of songs sung while cooking *harees*, a dish of wheat and meat, or songs sung while fetching wood.

But in addition to work-songs which were usually performed within a small group of women, there are individual songs sung in private, like lullabies for babies and children. Young girls also have their own special songs.

Only two forms of singing were performed in public by Qatari women, each on a different occasion and by a different group in society. The first was *al moradah*. This was usually done during the week that preceded the two Muslim feasts *'Eid al-Fitr* which follows *Ramadan*, and *'Eid al-Adha* after the pilgrimage to Mecca. Women and girls used to go to a place in the desert far away from the city, where they danced and sang without being seen by men. They would dress in their best embroidered clothes, and women of all social classes took part, as this was the only occasion when they shared such a public gathering.

The young women, aged between thirteen and fifteen, were the ones who performed the dance and sang, while the older women sang along with them. In this form of singing, girls stood in two rows facing each other. One row would sing a verse and then the other row would repeat it. Hence the name *al moradah* which means 'repeated'. The dance movements followed the drum beats, and the girls would move forward and backward in a rhythmic way. The songs sung during *al moradah* were of varied themes reflecting the social situation at the time; they sang of the bright moon whose light was the only guide for divers searching for pearls. They sang songs which described the beauty and good manners of girls whose hands were decorated with henna, and so on. The girls also sang songs which reflected their hidden desires for marriage, bearing in mind that this gathering was considered a good chance for the older women to choose a suitable bride for their sons. A song illustrating this says, "I wish I were a lemon in the hands of 'Abdul Rahman to be peeled by 'Abdullah and eaten by Salman." In *al moradah*, they also sang some of the songs that were popular in wartime and which revealed the true tribal attitude in the face of aggressors when everyone is united under one leader.

This form of singing was abandoned a long time ago by Qatari women. When I interviewed Mr Naser Al 'Othman, editor-in-chief of the prominent Arabic newspaper *Al Rayyah* and ex-director of the Arts and Culture Department, he had this to say: "The last *moradah* I saw was in 1952 or 53 ... you see, women didn't like being seen by men when they were dancing and singing. Of course, it was a small community where everyone knew one another and respected women's desires for privacy ... but now there's no privacy at all. They say that it was an incident when a young man drove his car in between the singing girls which made them indignant, and they've never had *al moradah* since. Mind you, the Ministry of Information has been trying to revive this tradition, and was able to supervise such an activity last year in one of the Doha's public parks, where men were kept out." So, *al moradah* disappeared as a result of the social changes which made other forms of art become more widely accepted.

The second form of collective public singing is *al 'ashori*, which is the name given to folk songs for wedding parties. *'Ashori* itself means "companionship", and because this is an essential part of marriage, marriage songs were called after it. It was and still is performed by the poorer class of Qatari women, who are descendants of slaves of African origin brought to the area during the nineteenth century. These women were able to take up singing as a profession because they were not subjected to the close scrutiny of society. We must stress here that, through centuries of Arab dynasties, it was the slave girls of varied origins who were involved in public entertainment, since it was a disgrace for free women to take up such a profession.

In addition to the absence of social restrictions, these women, who later formed professional groups of singers, dancers and percussionists, have a musical ability inherited from their ancestors. Like the great influence negro music had on jazz, soul and blues and rock and roll in America, negro rhythm also left an obvious imprint on some forms of singing in Qatar, as well as on dances and instruments. Even in the distant past slave girls made an obvious impact on Arabic music. The *mawal*, for instance, is a very famous form of colloquial poetry sung with the accompaniment of one musical instrument and is believed to have been invented by a slave girl in 805 AD during the caliphate of Harun Al Rashid.

The basic instruments used in *'ashori* songs are two percussion instruments, *al daf*, a tambourine, and *al tabl*, a kind of drum, also known to have come from Africa and used in all forms of Qatari folk music. *'Ashori* songs usually reflect the joy of the marriage occasion, and are always based on *nabati* verse;

> *"Tonight is a night of joy for everyone,*
> *The mother of the bridegroom invites the relatives*
> *Her heart is full of happiness and joy*
> *Tonight is the night of congratulations and*
> *   singing."*

Other songs are descriptions of the bridegroom, the bride's beauty, dress, jewellery, good family and so on. This is an example of one of many *'ashori* songs which are full of symbolic references:

> *"Morning has dawned … oh it has.*
> *What to do with him who forgets his promise*
> *Where is he, whom I've waited long for?"*

This song includes a hidden call for people to leave the bride and groom, by hinting that morning has dawned.

There are several female groups who perform in public, at gatherings or wedding celebrations, parties and so on. I was able to meet some of them. Asmaa Bint Harib is the leader of a group called *Najmat al Fajir*. Like other *'ashori* singers, she cannot read or write, and learnt her profession from her uncle and brother, who have their own folk groups. Zahra Bint Mgali is another leader of a different female group; she can perform different types of songs: *khamari* and *la'buni*, but not *'ashori*. She says she is too young to know how *'ashori* singing is performed and told me that she inherited her talent from her father.

La'buni songs are *nabati* verse with themes describing platonic love. *Khamari* songs, which are also a form of sung *nabati* verse, express love in a softer, more timid style, which male poets and singers do not favour, as it reveals weakness in love.

When they perform at a marriage ceremony, Zahra collects all the members of her group and takes them to the bride's house. When they enter the house, they drink coffee and then start singing. There is usually no prior training or preparation needed. As for payment, it is completely up to the bride's family to pay whatever they wish.

However, these folk music groups, male and female, are taken care of by the Department of Culture and Arts at the Ministry of Information, through whom a monthly salary is designated for each member, and help and guidance is provided.

The National Folk Music Group includes young Qatari women, aged from thirteen to sixteen, who for the first time sing and dance on stage with no veils covering their faces. They performed on stage for a mixed audience on February 22nd 1981 and 1982. This group was well received, and in 1982 Qatari girls also presented a sample of *al moradah* on stage.

As far as individual singing is concerned, there has been hitherto only one professional female singer, Amani Al 'Abdullah. As for Qatari actresses, they are few in number and the first time an actress, Mariam Rashid, appeared on stage was in 1974, in a play entitled *The Ghost House*. Nowadays, Widad 'Abdul Lateef is the only dedicated actress, who believes that the Qatari theatre still does not reflect people's problems, and that it is still trying to find the message it wants to convey.

Literature

In the history of Arab culture, women's contributions to literature have been greatly influenced by the varying social conditions as well as having been true reflections of them. A quick historic review of Arab women's role in this field, with emphasis on the Arabian peninsula, is necessary to avoid drawing exaggerated inferences when we explore Qatari women's contributions in the same sphere.

Poetry

From pre-Islamic times poetry has been the literary genre *par excellence*. It was an integral part of everyday life where social and intellectual trends were clearly reflected and from which researchers could draw many historical inferences. For an Arab, poetry was not only an individual means of expressing his innermost feelings and fulfilling an inherent talent, but more of a verbal art that performed much-needed social functions, like expressing the status of a tribe, and glorifying its courage, generosity and other attributes. Each tribe prided itself on having a renowned poet within its ranks. At the time, ancient tradition was passed on to future generations through the social function of classical poetry. This gave rise to its basic themes of love, satire, description, and lament. Underlying these lyric forms is the classical definition of poetry as "metrical, rhymed speech indicating a meaning". The ideal balance between a beautiful form and an excellent meaning in poetic expression was the aim of every poet. The power of the poem lay in its directness and expressiveness of things seen and observed more in the outside world than in the poet's own subjective visions.

Renowned poetesses dealt with most of classical poetry's aims or themes and followed the same literary forms, but in pre-Islamic times they concentrated on the theme in which they excelled; lament or *ritha'*. In this form the poem functioned as a mournful obituary, which overemphasized the different attributes of the dead. In it women lamented the death of male relatives only. This was a direct result of the social conditions of a tribal community, where man was the courageous defender of the tribe and woman was the recipient of his care and protection. Within such a culture, roles were set so that man was tough and daring, whilst woman was weak and sentimental. Thus men were not permitted to reveal their sentiments in poetry as this was considered weakness of character, although many poets have expressed their sentiments in love poetry. Lament poetry, however, remained the speciality of poetesses. Obviously the social function of this form of poetry affected the literary output of the poetesses of the time.

In the Islamic period *ritha'* lost its role and significance to the religious teachings which changed people's view of death and prohibited idolatry of the dead. This in turn reflected on women who became able to practise more freedom in Muslim society. During the golden age of the eighth century, women like Sakina, daughter of Al Hussein and granddaughter of the prophet Mohammed, and 'Aisha Bint Talha were able to contribute a lot to literary and cultural life through their literary salons. Social conditions then enabled poets to deal with varied topics, thus giving birth to the great tradition of classical Arabic poetry: the religious, political, and amatory compositions of the early Umayyad poets, the lyrics of the Andalusians, the mystical poetry of the *Sufis*, and the great classics of the 'Abbasids. The destruction of the 'Abbasid dynasty in the thirteenth century by the Mongols started a long period of literary stagnation and decay which lasted until the latter half of the nineteenth century, when Arabic literature as a whole began to revive in response to internal reform and the challenge of Western influence. Only then were Arab women able to venture into new literary fields, such as journalism and letter and story writing.

Turning our attention to the Arabian peninsula, one cannot overstress that the literature of a given period is not identified merely by the set of existing literary works, but equally by existing literary values. The interrelationship between the historical succession of norms of literary criticism and of literary works is important for an understanding of the present situation in the Gulf, where critics, acting as the carriers of literary norms, set forth requirements which are afterwards met by literary creation.

Nabati verse

Focusing on orally-composed and transmitted art, we find that, in addition to the classical forms of poetry, there also existed a less celebrated, though equally important, form of poetic expression known in Arabia as *nabati* verse. Originally, it had been tied to classical poetry, but in time became a more colloquial mode of expression. It is believed this resulted from the intermingling with non-Arabs, and in fact the word *nabati* comes from the naturalized "Nabateans", who lived in Iraq and southern Palestine. Their language differed considerably from classical Arabic. Exterior influences from other naturalized Arabs continued from the fifth century AH. The famous scholar Ibn Khaldoun cites examples of similar forms of poetry which were popular in North Africa. And yet there are no definite references, dates or reasons for the change that came over classical poetry in this area, and why it made way for this particular form of colloquial verse.

Nevertheless, *nabati* verse is not synonymous with popular rhyme, which is composed by simple people who remain anonymous. *Nabati* verse has known origins, and poems of famous *nabati* minstrels are memorized and live on through different generations. Perhaps more importantly, *nabati* verse is the only form of literature which has succeeded in uniting all classes of society. Normally, the elite never took part in the customs of commoners, but *nabati* verse was highly valued and its exponents greatly respected by both. At the same time, this verse form was the only creative outlet for the people who lived in the desert, and various poems would describe environmental problems as well as human ones. Perhaps most important of all, *nabati* verse was the only means of obtaining information at the time, and functioned more or less as the mass media do nowadays.

In *nabati* verse, the poet usually mastered the colloquial Gulf dialect, and enjoyed the full liberty of adding new words to create a rhyme, even though such words may not have been linguistically correct. This simplified matters for men and women who had little education, if indeed any, and enabled them to compose *nabati* poems for varied purposes.

In its infancy *nabati* verse adhered to the meter or *taf'il* rhyme, and unity of classical Arab poetry, but disregarded the grammatical rules of the language. This was not deliberate, but *nabati* poets came from the same bedouin environment that gave birth to Arabic poetic tradition. Yet, in time, meter, rhyme and unity too were subject to change as they were subject to different forces, the most effective of which was the poet's full liberty to improvise. Defining and documenting the innumerable meters and rhymes of *nabati* verse, has so far proved an impossible task for researchers in the field, because of the verse's reliance on oral transmission. Obviously because of this and because it dealt with varied topics, *nabati* verse was strongly attached to some singing forms and was thus preserved and transported from one area to another. It also performed an important role as part of the literature of the resistance against imperialistic forces. In this respect, Sheikh Qassim Bin Mohammed Al Thani's verses were quite influential and widespread as expressions of the growing protest against critical social and political conditions in Qatar as well as in the Gulf area.

Even though most *nabati* poets were men, a reasonable number of women were involved in composing this kind of verse for different purposes. These women poets usually recited their poems at women's gatherings, and other women present at these functions would immediately memorize the lines. In Qatar *nabati* verse by women has never been published, and in fact collecting it is still one of the most difficult challenges any researcher in folklore is likely to come across. Most *nabati* poetesses are women who would never have had their verses published, and in addition to this the women's gatherings, where *nabati* verse was recited and thus memorized, have now almost completely vanished.

Few Qatari women under forty years old are still interested in this form of poetic expression. The media have taken over and *nabati* verse programmes can either be heard on radio or watched on television. Newspapers also dedicate pages to *nabati* verse and Hamad Hassan Al Nu'emi, an authority on the subject, is in charge of the *nabati* verse page in the *Al Rayyah* newspaper. In search of further sources of information, I interviewed him but he had acquired little material so far. Hamad had a book on *nabati* poetesses in the Arabian peninsula, but nothing specific on Qatar as yet. Nevertheless, he went to great efforts and pointed out to me that most of the children's lullabies had been composed by women. Also, the *khamari* songs are based on *nabati* verse. I include a sample:

> *"Walk on, shepherd of camels.*
> *Ahmed lives in the valley, with no food or drink,*
> *The Arabs are respectable in white, I respectable*
>   *in black;*
> *The Arabs slaughter sheep, and for you I*
>   *slaughter my heart,*
> *God save my son and let him become a happy*
>   *man."*

Naturally, a translation into English destroys the original intrinsic value of the poetry. In this song, whose purpose is to send a child to sleep, one can detect certain religious allusions. Ahmed is a symbol of the Prophet, and there is a reference to pilgrimage procedures whereby people dress in white for the occasion. There is also the conviction that black is the respectable colour for women, meaning the overveil. The short poem ends with a prayer to God to save the woman's child.

Modern writing

Nabati verse was the basic literary form in which Qatari women participated before the oil boom. The mid-fifties marked the time in which the Gulf area began to feel the increasing winds of cultural change. This resulted from the greater political and economic interest in the area, the increase in imported labour, the presence of regular air-travel links with Arab and Western countries, and the setting-up of local newspapers, magazines and other media such as radio and television. The literary output of poetry, songs, articles and stories reflected the conflicts brought about by the new prosperity and accompanying change. That period is considered by some critics as a period of authentic cultural composition. The oil boom followed and brought with it more influences on the cultural scene, but interest in the new consumer society was profit-motivated and a mixture of good and bad found a market for itself. The impact of such influences, internal as well as external, has not yet produced what could be termed as a new Gulf culture.

In Qatar the mid-sixties and early seventies were times of change; in 1968 radio started transmission and television followed in 1970. The first two magazines *Al Doha* and *Al 'Oroba* were published in the same year. The role of the media in creating new social awareness of world issues was felt in Qatar at a time when education as well as political change were making an impact on its cultural life.

Mai Salem was the first woman writer to publish

articles in these local magazines in 1970. She didn't use a pen-name. Other women followed suit, and up to today more women's names continue to appear offering articles, short stories, poetry or essays to newspapers and magazines. Many Gulf newspapers and magazines like to print women's writings since they give the publications a modern image; hence the chance to publish is easily attainable for most women writers. This could, on the other hand, be a disadvantage as it allows for works to be published prematurely.

Yet the competition is on the increase; this and time are the decisive factors that will determine which of these writers will continue to mature, develop and contribute something to Arabic literature, and which will just fade away after practising a mere time-consuming hobby.

The Arab women writers and poetesses of the early twentieth century were busy establishing women's associations and magazines in Egypt, Syria and Lebanon. They were greatly influenced by the prevailing national and social currents. That is why their efforts centred mainly on liberating women from ignorance, reforming prisons, helping the poor, glorifying the role of family and motherhood and so on. At the same time, other contemporary Arab writers and poetesses used the pen to present their demands and reflect women's problems and ambitions.

Qatari women started on the same lines, but developed into the contemporary stage of expression, in subject if not in style and literary ability. When we explore their varied works, we find that no matter what the subject matter is they still possess the "lament" theme of early Arab poetesses. This theme manifests itself in their style which sometimes reflects helplessness, sadness or despair. Maysah Al Kholeifi is a young poetess, who publishes her poems in newspapers. Her poem *Greenery and the Friendly Voice* shows this inherent theme of "lament" at the beginning but seems to free itself from feelings of negative helplessness in the latter part where a more positive and symbolic stand is taken. The poem was published in *Al Rayyah* in February, 1981.

I remembered you ... beloved one,
With pain sapping my days,
Lying within my soul ... strangling it,
And putting an end to my dreams.

I remembered the treacherous world ... its
cruelty,
And how it disturbed my brightness and my sweet
melodies,
I recalled how the treacherous world
Threw its darkness on me,
And when I sat shaking ... and tasted silence and
exile
Then ... your eager voice tempted me to live
And relinquish my fears when I meet you.

Like clear water your green voice made happy my
day
And covered me with its tenderness, asked me
about love.
Love, I said, is to cherish dreams in the heart,
And not fear the walls, or the anger of the
hurricane,
Love is to wake up ... to bypass every siege
That parts us for a while ... And not fear walking
through fire,
And forgetting those unhappy shadows from the
past.
So don't stay away from the soul ... Come to meet
me
And we'll kick away ... the world of yesterday.

Maysah's poem is written in free verse. Translating it into English destroys a lot of its intrinsic meaning yet it is not my intention to evaluate such work since this should be the duty of critics.

It is worth pointing out here that the free verse movement in the Arab world is thought to have been subject to Western influence. In their book *An Anthology of Modern Arabic Poetry*, M.A. Khouri and H. Al Gar stressed that, despite the fact that Arabic poetry has come closer to Western poetry, it has never relinquished its own character and originality. The influence of the West pointed out new directions and awakened poets to new methods, new ideas and new possibilities. Free verse rejected the traditional rules of Arabic poetry such as meter, *taf'il*, rhyme and unity in favour of freer, simpler poetic language. Free verse is capable of a more vital expression of content through the intensity of the artistic process and the imaginative use of words, metaphors, symbols, imagery, dramatic monologues and other devices. This content ranges from universal, philosophical questions about the human condition – life, death, love and salvation – to the particular social and cultural issues and situations characteristic of the poet's own time, vision and experiences.

Obviously, despite what some critics believe to be many high walls and obstacles standing between Qatari women and writing, the process has begun, and the traps of the consumer society where Western fashion shops and beauty salons vie in exporting tempting modern trends have not completely succeeded in diverting women's attention from the basic issues they should be writing about in the 1980's.

But what were the prevailing themes until the late seventies, when more controversial issues followed, such as discussion of traditions that hinder positive development and change, education abroad, the redundant veil and so on?

Kaltham Gaber was amongst the pioneers, she published her first short story in *Al 'Oroba* magazine

in 1973. Kaltham was the first Qatari woman writer
to publish a major work, a collection of short stories
which she wrote between 1973 and 1978. The book,
entitled *You and The Echoing Forest of Silence and
Hesitation* was received with many exaggerated inferences when it came out. Some saw it as a symbol of
the suffering of Arab women, while others judged it
harshly, comparing it to classical works of literature
and stamping it as a failure.

A famous critic Mohammed Gaber Al Ansari explored Kaltham's work and evaluated it on a different
basis. To him the book does allude to some of the
existing social restrictions, even though it can hardly
be described as a work that symbolizes the suffering
of Qatari women.

Most of the stories centre round one theme: the
man/woman relationship. And, despite the fact that
love has always been one of the basic themes of
stories and poems in Arabic literature, a natural
result of the separation of the sexes, Al Ansari rules
out the idea that the central problem in Kaltham's
book is this relationship and the problem of unsuccessful love. "If we examine the kind of relationships
which the writer presents in her stories and connect
them to the present chain of Qatar's sociological
development and the nature of women's role in it, we
find that the author was able to reveal the following
dilemma. Qatari girls live in a modern world. Girls
watch love stories on television, read books, travel
and are subject to different forces which should
change their lifestyle, yet the girls are forced to
accept that such a life is not yet permissible in their
society. A chain of numerous negative reactions
follows: helplessness, failure and frustration."

In her stories Kaltham reflects a weak emotional
image of the inexperience of woman at this stage; the
"lament" mentality also persists in such early writings. Kaltham's intention was to explore and expose

such problems without imposing solutions:

> *I was afraid to tell him anything. Weeping was my only relief, and because I found comfort in his compassion, I let my head pillow against his shoulder feeling a delicious, sleepless dream take over me. I was not used to dancing with anyone except my father. What will he think of me after this? I had not consulted him. I was unable to say no ... the dance ended and we returned a second time. I wished I was no longer aware of him. Now, in his presence, the chains tied me anew – I wanted to run away. My eyes caught those of my father who was looking for me. I breathed a sigh of relief. I hid behind my father taking his arm, fleeing from the dream that tied me ...*

The father takes his daughter to a party, leaves her alone and searches for her at the end to take her home. During this time, she meets and admires a man of forty known as "The Impossible" because she knows full well that any relationship between them really is impossible. There is hence a conflict between customs and new situations, when the father places his daughter in a new atmosphere, leaving her lost and a target for different influences. He then takes her home, having exposed her to a situation she could not possibly handle. As for the writer's style, her language is in between prose and poetry. It suits the nature of her topic, and is in harmony with female notions and indeed the author was in her teens when she wrote this particular story. One critic even described it as nothing more than a personal confession, an interior monologue, which takes the shape of a story.

But what does Kaltham herself think of her work? When I asked her, she said she was not entirely satisfied with her stories, and that she believed they reflected both her position as a young woman and the social structure. She admits that she has matured since then, and that her writings now avoid this obsession with the man/woman relationship, and the emotive personal style. Kaltham has read all the well-known Arab writers, and translations of Western authors. She particularly admires the works of Emile Zola, Somerset Maugham, Alberto Moravia, Simone de Beauvoir, Pearl Buck, Charles Dickens and Albert Camus.

Kaltham is a calm yet determined young woman, who after nearly ten years of writing knows she is still maturing and that there is still a great deal to learn and write about. Literary tendencies seem to run in her family – her father was a *nabati* poet. Born in 1958 Kaltham now studies at Qatar University's Social Services Department, because this is the only field where she can be close to people's problems and sufferings and be of assistance to them both directly through her job, and indirectly by writing about such topics.

Kaltham's more recent writings clearly show a change in theme and subject matter, along with a more mature style, where her use of imagery and metaphors create a more effective atmosphere in a story that tries to free itelf from the interior monologue which seems to prevail in women's writings in Qatar.

In her story published in the renowned *Al Doha* magazine in November 1981, *Milad Gadid (A New Birth)* the writer tries to escape from reality into a different imaginary world. She describes the heroine's total dependence on her family, and her constant desire to break away from their influence. The heroine's search for a new identity is traced through a total rejection of all aspects of her present identity but she cannot detach herself from her family, who symbolize society's controls imposed on the individual.

Kaltham commences her story, *A New Birth*, by
rejecting the whole idea of having a definite identity
and later on she explicitly expresses such a rejection:

> *Why go back? Money, a suitcase, a name. Why*
> *should one have an identity, one mother and one*
> *father? Why should such ties exist? They choke*
> *me like a chain and I don't want to belong ... or*
> *go back ...*

Here Kaltham also says that human beings are
alike and that superficial differences (name, identity,
etc.) should be ignored.

The story begins when the heroine travels with her
family to Paris, but decides not to take any luggage.
With the first signs of dawn she sneaks out of the hotel
and spends the entire day roaming through the
streets of Paris, refuting her identity and connections
to any particular place. She is hungry, doesn't have
money for food but does not care.

Night eventually falls and she sleeps in a park.

> *Suddenly, I wake up ... darkness surrounds me*
> *... and frightens me ... oh, fear has conquered*
> *my movements, shaken my self-confidence and*
> *swept away my hunger and exhaustion. I want to*
> *go back ... my scream echoes in the park and*
> *tears build up in my chest ... I want to go back ...*
> *the steps behind me persist, and I'm afraid of this*
> *darkness and the hurrying footsteps behind me ...*
> *mother, father, I want to go back. ... But in Paris*
> *there is no straight route leading back to the hotel*
> *... and I am a stranger ...*

So, despite the heroine's impulsive desire to
escape, she is not ready yet to face the alien society
she has thrown herself into. The dilemma persists;
the social bond is greater than her ability to break
away from it, because the bond is within her. Her
dependence on a protector (father or family) still
persists.

Noura Al Saad is a newcomer who began publishing her articles and short stories in 1980. She is thought to have a promising talent that will definitely make its mark on Gulf women's literature. Noura's style is quite articulate and mature, despite her limited experience. Yet some of her early pieces are like Kaltham Gaber's, more monologues than short stories. In a short article entitled *In Search of a Face* Noura expresses the same problem of identity.

> *I am female ... so I'm nothing. I hold my pen and write ... in the darkness of the night I write ... so that I don't see what I'm writing ... and get scared. I take the first train ... ask for a one-way ticket ... and sit in it hoping it travels into no place and no truth ... Don't ask me about my name ... my stop ... when I'm coming back or where I'm going ... because I don't know.*

Noura's expressions and figurative language are similar to Kaltham's while her choice of subject-matter is quite forthright.

In her short story *Your Ivory Claws Killed Me* published in *Al Rayyah* in March 1981, Noura discusses women's position versus man.

The use of imagery is very powerful in this story, which is a description of a male falcon hunting a pigeon, the strong versus the weak. The eagle and the dove are the most familiar pair of bird contrasts in international women's literature. The frightening aspect of the bird metaphor dominates this story.

> *He reaches out as if he reads her mind ... but as if he controls each and every movement she makes, manipulates her attitudes. She even gives in ... (this stupid female doesn't know how to rebel against males).*

Self-assertion remains the basic theme of many
stories, poems and articles, and, in an even more
mature short story published in 1981 in *Al Doha*
magazine, Noura stresses self-assertion (in the right
context) in defiance of male supremacy. Under the
title *The Dream and the Waiting* she hints at more
than one important problem in a busy working
mother's life.

> *Despite her eyes which ache as if full of pins, she*
> *couldn't sleep (between being awake and the*
> *dream is a small distance which doesn't allow*
> *easy breathing ... that is why she doesn't sleep,*
> *doesn't dream....)*

The heroine is a teacher who loves painting, but
whose husband does not encourage her to practise
her hobby. But in school there are more problems for
other teachers:

> *Oh, those were the days when we dreamt and*
> *waited, waited for the future, and here is that*
> *future, a load of exercise books, a load of troubles,*
> *a load of washing.*

At least this teacher decides while listening to her
colleague not to let her dream of becoming a painter
die:

> *What is the use of fear, hesitation and escape?*
> *She hurries to the store, picks up the paints, puts*
> *her nails in them, and on that board things start*
> *to shape themselves with meanings behind them.*
> *The world is nil, but not inside her. The phone*
> *rings but she doesn't care. She has finally found*
> *the other woman she once gave up."*

Unlike Kaltham's heroines, Noura's heroine in this
story is a more positive character, whose search for

identity does not prove to be futile or meaningless, but leads to fulfilment of her ambitions. Defiance also is not an aim in itself but a means of achieving one's aims.

When it comes to the issue of women's rights Noura is quite outspoken, and in an article published in *Al Rayyah* she discussed the problems of being a teenager:

> *The barricades surrounding a girl, from an overveil and a veil, have been designed to protect her and defend her honour. Everything, everybody, all customs and traditions, all society's institutions are dedicated and programmed to protect and control her actions, but shouldn't we concentrate on building her own sense of good and bad? When she goes to school, the girl mixes with all kinds of personalities and cannot herself distinguish black from white. Being a teenager is difficult enough, so how about future and more difficult challenges like marriage and bringing up children?*

Noura goes on stressing that it is the girl's duty as well as society's to be up to the challenges of a different way of life, where some of the old traditions are completely redundant.

Loulowah Al Misnid is a different kind of writer, even though she started on the same note of reflecting personal conflicts in her early writings. She started writing poetry and small articles at school, and then won third place in a school competition for short stories. Loulowah is a graduate of Kuwait University's Faculty of Economics and Political Science. She now works in the Humanities Research Centre of Qatar University.

Loulowah was one of two women who represented Qatar in the second regional conference on the status of Gulf women, which was held in Kuwait in 1981.

The other woman who attended was Mariam Darwish who is in charge of the Women's Branch of the
Qatar Red Crescent Society. Loulowah's writings are
mainly articles and researches that serve a definite
purpose: for instance, educational policies and how
effective they are in increasing the economic productivity of a Qatari woman.

In one article, published in *Al Doha*, she talked to
several Qatari women assistant lecturers, and discussed the issue of their productivity at the university. She concludes that more options should be available on the work-front and more facilities for working
women to upgrade the value of women's work in
Qatari society. Loulowah is a promising journalist
who knows which subjects to touch on, and how to
deal with them.

Loulowah uses her own name like Kaltham and
Noura when she signs her articles. In addition to her
spontaneous personality she is a more sophisticated
article writer than her colleagues, but she humbly
rules out such views, saying that for literature there is
one basic prerequisite and that is to represent social
phenomena, mostly negative ones, in an effort either
to bring them to light or find a solution to them.

In her short story *Thick Fog and Agony*, published
in December 1980 in *Al Doha* magazine, Loulowah
describes the same issue of the rejection of society's
traditions in the heroine's character. She marries a
salesman next door for the wrong reasons.

> *When I finished at primary school and wanted to*
> *pursue my education, my father had to agree, my*
> *mother, uncles and brothers too. My brother said*
> *then: When the girl is educated she becomes a*
> *human being. Here she is a female ... just a*
> *female ...*

But the heroine defies her family and when her
friends come to visit she screams at one of them:

> *You've come here with your university degree,*
> *boasting about your beliefs in women's rights*
> *and how you voiced your opinion that women*
> *have a leading role in liberating the Third World,*
> *but your degree is worthless. When I was sinking*
> *you didn't do anything to save me and after all the*
> *verbal fighting you've been doing . . . you've*
> *decided to be female.*

Loulowah continues:

> *After the truth had struck them, they took off. She*
> *slammed the door, held her long dress and jumped*
> *in the air like an outraged horse . . . running with*
> *the air slamming her cheeks . . . oh, she loves this*
> *thrust into the air . . . it removes the thick fog of*
> *agony from her inside . . .*

Among the younger generation we also find Qatari girls who show a definite literary talent. The writings of Zahra Yousif Al Malki show a natural choice of subject. Her story *Tears Shed* begins with the tiring search for the secret of existence.

> *Raindrops fall on the window and a lovely silence*
> *hovers over the room . . . from time to time the sun*
> *shines from between the clouds and the rich*
> *words are imprisoned in me. The letters and the*
> *words are heaped inside me. But who am I? And*
> *what am I? A dream or a reality? A ghost or a*
> *human being? Me . . . this word with scattered*
> *letters always wounds me. It stands in front of me*
> *like a high mountain which I cannot climb. I try*
> *to know who I am. My identity? My dreams? My*
> *address? my reality? and questions multiply*
> *while answers remain far from reach.*

Personal conceptions are mixed up with events and dialogue, but the personal side is clearly stressed. The ego continues to be the centre: the writer does not abide by the principles of short story writing.

Another rising talent is Bahia 'Abdul Rahman Al Baker whose writing abides by story-writing rules, but whose style is less mature. Her story *Between Two Worlds* deals with the conflict which an Arab who goes to the West experiences. He is faced with a strange world, different from his, in which he is exposed to the loss of his identity.

> *Strange this world to which he has come...*
> *Everything in it is delicious and exciting. Where*
> *had he been all these years? He was carried away*
> *with troubles and events in that dead land. He*
> *was away from this open society. He feels disgust*
> *when he remembers the farmers in his country*
> *and the girls' thick and coarse hands. But here,*
> *there's dancing and fun... What an exciting life!*
> *Let him try this coloured liquid in bottles. He was*
> *about to fall, but some hidden thing stopped him*
> *before it was too late.*

Through reading excerpts of Qatari women's writings we find that the search for an identity remains the obsession of women in a quickly-changing world. Who is the "Qatari woman" as opposed to all the other women, Arab and foreign, who flood into the country with their own ways and attitudes? What should it be like when she travels abroad? Should she do away with traditions, and can she? This cultural turmoil is natural, and in the face of strong winds of change, Qatari identity must be preserved.

A final word on this issue is that Arab women as well as Qatari women live in different environmental, social and economic conditions from their Western counterparts, and are still subject to contradictory social conditions. Cultural awareness remains relative, and judging them by European standards would be quite irrelevant.

Nevertheless I would like to quote here Patricia Meyer Spacks's description of the artist as a woman:

> *Like the adolescent, the artist is a dreamer and a revolutionary; like the adolescent, he often finds his accomplishment inadequate to his imaginings. But his dream, setting him apart, helps him to escape the burden of the real. To some women, as to some men, the idea of art seems to solve all problems. They may insistently describe themselves as artists without actually creating much art, using the self-designation to express wish rather than fact, trying to transform reality by refusing to accept the given conditions of life as when they write about themselves directly, as many have done, they reveal the complete purpose that the condition of being an artist may serve.*

CHAPTER SIX

Qatari Women at Work – Achievements and Effects

In the West, work has been the focal issue in the history of the women's liberation movement. Differences in pay, discrimination against women in the workplace and in employment led feminist leaders into the long struggle for equal opportunities. As their ranks grow, women in the labour force are reshaping both home and jobs, they have brought changes in everything from eating habits to the institution of marriage. In the Arab world the relatively recent but steady flow of women out of the home and into the labour force has caused similar, though not so profound effects on their society.

Like all complex social changes, the going-to-work movement in Qatar was shaped by cultural and economic forces. The growth of education and the widening of its scope, the affluence brought by oil revenues, the contact with other societies and the role of the mass media in changing traditional concepts are all forces that acted positively in this respect. However, the accompanying problems differ both in size and nature from those facing Western women and society. For example, economists argue that the influx of women into the American labour force has aggravated unemployment. And while women's work has become acceptable by social standards, views differ on its economic value. In Gulf societies, the opposite is in effect, and most Gulf sociologists are calling for a significant increase in women's participation in the workforce. This, they say, would lessen their countries' dependence on foreign labour, and enable women to contribute to the current ambitious development schemes. In this chapter, I propose to explore the reasons that motivate Qatari women to work, the cultural forces that make it possible, equal opportunities, the implications of women's work at home, and the future role expected of Qatari women in the work force.

The role of education in providing new opportunities

Until 1955, when the first formal girls' school in Qatar was opened and headed by Amnah Mahmood Al Gidah, the position of Qatari women had remained unchanged for a long time. Only religious education was available, and paid work was almost unheard of. The idea of women's education was very controversial when it first came into existence, three years after the first official primary school opened for boys in 1952. Amnah, the first ever Qatari headmistress and probably the first female government employee, was fully aware of the social situation and general misapprehension, and had to devote much time and energy to fetching the girls from their houses and the more difficult task of convincing parents of the value and need for female education at that time. Amnah told me: "Most of the girls were prevented from attending school. People were against formal education because they believed it was anti-religious and corruptive. So, I used to explain to them how Islam considers education obligatory for both males and females who should seek it from the moment of birth until death."

When I met Amnah who is now retired with a Government pension, I was astonished by how enthusiastic she still felt about women's education, and how necessary she believed it to be in order to ameliorate women's social conditions. Married women had also wanted to join the school, but as Amnah explained, "We couldn't provide for them. The schools were for young girls, and we simply couldn't accept married women ... but I can still remember how they would come to me with their babies. It was a problem then; later on literacy and adult education programmes catered for most of these women."

The first girls' school was opened with the full support of the Ministry of Education as a primary school. In 1961, the first preparatory level was the highest standard officially permitted by the Ministry, but the school unofficially provided facilities for second preparatory, and this paved the way for official secondary schooling.

Education in all its manifestations is now one of the most important Government priorities, is highly sought after, and has developed both in quantity and quality. Originally, there was only one girls' school with 50 pupils, but according to the Ministry of Education's Annual Statistical Report of 1980/81, there are now 70 girls' schools with 19,356 students.

The University of Qatar was opened in 1973, offering two Faculties of Education, one for men and one for women, with 157 students, of which 103 were young women. Since then, four other faculties have been created (Science, Humanities, Islamic Studies and Engineering), and the number of female students has now reached 2285 compared to 1530 male students. 238 girls are abroad on scholarships, 26 studying for postgraduate degrees. The Government has provided equal educational opportunities for women, beginning the process of bringing them out of seclusion and encouraging their desire for higher education and work.

Despite all this, some Westerners still argue that Islam negatively influences girls' access to education. In answer to that, I feel a clear differentiation should be drawn between religion and culture. The example usually presented is that in Islamic countries early marriage of girls prevents their participation in secondary schooling. This is a cultural factor, as I explained in Chapter 3, and has been subject to change. Discrimination against girls and women in education is not a feature of the Qatari educational system. The curricula in male and female schools are the same, though ingrained tendencies obviously persist. Despite the Sex Discrimination Act of 1975, one could argue that in Britain there still exist certain inequalities in educational and consequently job opportunities. A relatively small number of girls, for example, study science and technology at school and university, thus few are sufficiently qualified to enter skilled jobs in industry. Similarly careers advice in schools is still very restricted, and most teachers still think in terms of certain ranges of careers for girls and others for boys. I only mention this to stress the fact that it will still take a long time before Qatari girls can widen their choice of subjects and careers, and subsequently study non-traditional topics.

Education in Qatar is free and readily available for both sexes, so parents do not have to bear the financial burden of providing knowledge for their children. Discrimination at the household level as to who should go to school, the boy or girl, because of the cost of schooling, does not exist. At one stage students were given monthly salaries by the government, increasing as the individual attained a higher level of education, in order to encourage both students and parents. Food and clothing was also provided, but nowadays only certain educational faculties receive such financial incentives (the science department in secondary schools, colleges of commerce and industry, and religious and teachers' institutes). The monthly salaries range between 500 and 1,000 Qatari Riyals. Stationery, transportation, clothing and so on are still provided free for all students (whether Qatari or not) who attend schools.

With regard to Qatari women expanding their choice of subject matter, Loulowah Al Misnid's study on *Educational policies and their role in increasing women's productivity* is of particular interest. Loulowah is a graduate of Kuwait University's Faculty of Economics and Political Science, and now works in the Faculty of Humanities at Qatar University. She stressed the need for more variety and specialization at university level, as, according to her, this is an essential prerequisite for women's contribution to development. Most women graduate as qualified teachers (a trend that is also prevalent in the West), but there is an urgent necessity for women to devote their talents to other fields. The important process of industrialization requires a greater contribution from women in engineering and science generally. This cannot be achieved unless there is more diversification in the educational facilities at university level. On the vocational level, too, Loulowah calls for training women in skills other than sewing, embroidery and manual crafts, preferably concentrating on typing, photography, computer sciences, etc. She believes that the media could play a greater role in expressing the value of women's work, and help it become more socially acceptable.

Many women lecturers and graduates of Qatar University agree that discrimination between male and female students does not exist, except on the higher, postgraduate courses. Badriah Al Mollah wanted to complete her studies in the United States, hoping to obtain an MA in Educational Methods, but was unable to travel because she did not have a *mahraam*. This is a close male relative (father, brother or husband) who travels with a woman and stays with her until she finishes her education. According to an official of the Scholarships Department, "If girls study at a university which includes a boarding house for girls, they are allowed to go as long as the father agrees to it ... this has happened in some cases."

In education, this is really the only limitation on women. Social pressures are strongly in favour of imposing such religious restrictions. According to Law No. 9 (for 1976), however, the official stand is that all Qatari students are eligible for being sent abroad on scholarship, regardless of their sex. Moreover, according to an exception of the scholarships law (Section 30), an accompanying *mahraam* is entitled to an air ticket and the equivalent of sixty per cent of the woman's allowance which is paid by the Ministry of Education. There are now about 500 female Qatari university graduates. Seven of them have obtained Master's degrees. Two have doctorates, twenty are studying for MAs and six are studying for doctorates in Britain. Most of these female graduates go out to work.

Qatari women's entry into the job market

Under ideal circumstances, women's work in Islam is not necessary, because a woman should have no financial responsibilities whatsoever. For a wife, the husband is a provider; for a mother, her son; for a sister, the brother; for a daughter, the father and so on. If the woman has no relatives, then it is society's duty to look after her, or she may seek a job.

In the sixties and early seventies, Qatari women were simply not expected to go out and take jobs. Their basic role was believed to be in the house, as it was the husband's obligation to provide for the family. During this time, the women who did work were mainly the widowed or divorced. The early seventies was the time when social schemes and the developing educational process began to affect the nature as well as the pattern of women's work.

The changes brought about by affluence and education not only influenced society's attitudes to the idea of women working, but have basically provided a labour market for women. At first, most of the female labour was imported, as few Qatari women immediately entered the work force. Education was the starting point where most jobs became readily available; teaching was mainly undertaken by middle-class women, while the poorer classes worked as office maids (*farasha*) in schools. Some were employed to travel in school buses, where they would accompany girls to make sure they reached home safely while others sold nuts and sweets to students.

University graduates were ready by the mid-seventies to take over the teaching profession and also the hierarchy of school administration as part of the process of Qatarization. According to the Personnel Department's Annual Report of 1980, the proportion of Qatari women employed in education was over half the female work force (1317 out of 2233).

These statistics also show that the female work force employed by the Government is 3527 women of different nationalities representing 15 per cent of the total work force, which includes Qataris and non-Qataris. In 1975 the figure was 1646, so in five years it more than doubled. Keeping the Qatarization process in mind, it is reasonable to deduce that most of the increase came from the Qatari side. Qatari women now represent 14 per cent of the total Qatari work force.

Nowadays, most women seek employment; the younger generations from poorer classes who have profited from education take up jobs such as telephone switchboard operators, nursing and occupations which most middle-class women consider as being beneath them. As for women among the rich strata of society, they never worked in the past, and would rarely do so even nowadays. In Western societies the trend has been quite similar, whereby middle-class women began careers in education and social work, and married women worked only if their husbands were unable to support their families.

Changing social attitudes towards women's work cannot be ignored. In 1977, 185 male students from Qatar University were interviewed, and most were against descriptions that undervalued women, or placed them in a subservient role. The majority rejected the view that men are more intelligent than women, but the most significant replies concerned women's rights, where most answers favoured women's right to work and equal pay. Today, a good job is becoming more of a status symbol for a middle-class wife, and even for the few of the richer women who are seeking paid work. The percentage of women participating in the work force in Qatar, 15 per cent, might be considered insignificant when compared to some of the industrialized European countries, but to do so is unfair. Years ago, middle and upper class Western women, especially married ones, had many reasons for not working outside the family home, especially for fear of being ostracized by society.

It is also worth noting at this stage that unpaid work is not taken into consideration when compiling statistics on the percentage of women participating in the work force. Unpaid work has also been considered by many as irrelevant to the process of emancipation, as it does not provide women with financial independence. Nevertheless, a related United Nations report, issued recently by the Economic Commission in Africa, made clear that women's role in unpaid jobs cannot be undervalued in developing countries, where women shoulder 60 to 80 per cent of the workload in agriculture, in addition to their roles as housewives. The UN report underlines that in such cases women tend to be the real heads of the family. Developing societies, therefore, should not be evaluated by the same criteria which have originated in developed societies.

Equal opportunities – theory and social realities

In the late forties the French author Simone de Beauvoir published *The Second Sex*, a scholarly and comprehensive study of women's roles, past and present. The general tone of the work was one of regret for women's limited opportunities for fulfilment as human beings. It looked forward to a time when men and women, without denying their differences, could function as true equals. Since then, the feminist movement in Europe and the United States has accomplished a great deal but in some instances has also gone to unacceptable extremes. Over-emphasis on self-fulfilment and the decrying of the roles of wife and mother have provoked certain counter-reactions. In the United States, this has even led to the creation of anti-women's women's groups. This is the logical backlash to the stern feminist attitude which heavily attacks and undermines women who choose to remain at home and take care of their husbands and children. Perhaps most people are now suffering from the strange idea that unless an individual is generating his or her own income, he or she is totally useless to society, but with the current high unemployment figures, this is bound to change. In an article entitled *Wolves in Pigs' Clothing* published in the *Observer* in 1980, Katherine Whitehorn elaborated on this. In her part of Cambridge, Massachusetts, she explained,

*The first question anyone asks is 'What do you
do?', and if the answer is 'Well, nothing', they are
apt to look abstractedly over your head and drift
away – especially men.*

Among the basic reasons for the emergence of
feminism in England and America during the nineteenth century was that the job market opened up for
women as a result of the Industrial Revolution.
Women worked because they had to and thus accepted lower pay. Improving the conditions of working women was the field where women fought hard.
Financial rights were the basic worry of the feminist
movement, which sought and eventually won women
the right to own property, to vote, and later to receive
equal pay and job opportunities.

Despite the laws passed by the different governments to eliminate inequalities and, despite the
victories, there is still widespread discrimination
against women in the workplace. In Western countries the earnings gap between women and men still
exists. In the United States, for instance, women's
pay has increased significantly in recent years, but
not as fast as men's. Consequently, the difference
between men's and women's pay is greater today
than it was two decades ago. Even though these were
the findings of a Women's Bureau report in 1977,
drastic changes are not expected in that field. The
study also found that American women were over-
represented at the lower end of the pay scale. This
reflects the continued concentration of women in
relatively low-skilled, low-paying jobs.

In Britain in 1980 the percentage of women working in service industries was 75 per cent. Obviously
even for the liberated women in the developed world,
social pressures negatively affect the implementation
of laws which are to the advantage of women. Many
feminists explain that the problem lies not with the

anti-discrimination laws and regulations, but in inherent attitudes towards women.

In 1980 Britain's Women in the Media group met to assess the image of women in the media in an effort to stop Britain's newspapers, advertisements and magazines being sexist in the way they presented women. Most of my women interviewees (of different nationalities) supported the view that many men are still prejudiced against women in the West. The secretary trap, where many employers tend to shunt women into secretarial jobs, was also mentioned.

In fact, the Qatari woman entered the job market under completely different circumstances, when her society was enjoying the benefits of the oil boom and all the social welfare schemes that accompanied it. Exploitation of women at work has never existed since the time of new prosperity, especially as in most cases the economic need for a woman to work has never been the motivating factor. Social and psychological pressures led to work being considered as an acceptable outlet, freeing women from the domestic confines of the household and enabling them to make new acquaintances. Self-assertion featured as a basic drive for most of the emerging generations of Qatari women, who seek constantly to improve their status.

By 1976, the provisions of the Fundamental Qatari Constitution had already catered for women's rights. With regard to property: "A woman has the full right to have a financial status separate from and independent of that of her husband. Thus she has the right to own any kind of property, to administer and dispose of it, either by herself or through an agent." In this issue, Qatari law follows the Muslim *Shari'a* laws which are its fundamental source of legislation. In the past, women enjoyed all these rights and normally practised them through an agent. Nowadays, Qatari women own their own fashion shops, share the ownership of beauty salons, etc. The need to overemphasize this right simply does not exist, as it has been always acknowledged by Islam in theory and in practice.

Equality in job opportunities and equal pay are the issues that aroused a great deal of interest in my Western interviewees. Such equalities have been guaranteed by Law No. 9 (1976), which stipulates that:

> *A woman has the equal right as a man to be*
> *appointed to any government job, and enjoy its*
> *benefits such as salary, leaves and allowances.*

This law also takes into consideration the special status of a working woman, and provides her with paid maternity leave of one month. Curiously, if we explore the social realities of this situation, we find, as Mr Mobarak Al Khater, Director of the Legal Affairs Department, put it: "Qatari law is ahead of society's thinking. It provides for equal work opportunities which are sometimes not available if traditions prevent them. But there is definitely no discrimination against Qatari women when it comes to the financial aspects of salary, leave etc." If we examine the facts and figures presented by the Personnel Department in its Annual Report of 1980, it becomes clear that the percentage of Qatari women represented at the higher end of the pay scale is almost 70 per cent, compared with the percentage of Qatari men represented which amounts to almost 30 per cent. In fact, 1148 Qatari women out of the whole Qatari female work force, 1614 women, are employed at senior grades, receiving senior salaries and allowances.

Work patterns during the sixties reflected the available opportunities – especially in education and nursing – at a time when the government was concentrating its efforts on building the country's infrastructure and planning for an ever-increasing standard of welfare and social services. The growing numbers of female students and the opening of new schools provided a big labour market for women, one which was not disagreeable to the prevalent traditions. Teaching and learning in general are highly regarded in Arab and Muslim countries, where proverbs go to such extremes as saying "He who teaches me one letter, enslaves me". Because the teaching profession has always been considered as highly respectable, women were and still are encouraged to enter into it. But, as Amnah Mahmood says: "There are increasing numbers of girls graduating from university, and we have enough teachers ... more than enough ... so there's really no place for new graduates in this profession, and they'll have to find employment in other fields, or their education will have been in vain." Segregation of the sexes, which originally paved the way to entering such professions, can be maintained at school level, but as one Qatari headmistress pointed out: "We are not totally segregated from the administration in the Ministry. We have regular meetings with male officials where we discuss educational policies, achievements, problems and so on ... so, even in education, things are changing."

In the past customs and traditions hindered most women from contemplating joining the labour force unless there was a pressing financial need. "It was considered shameful," as one of my male interviewees put it, "for a man to let his wife work for money, it meant he was not able to provide for her and was thus considered socially inferior." These customs have been considerably toned down, but ideas related to the segregation of sexes in the workplace sometimes still continue. The upper classes certainly believe that a woman working with a man is unthinkable as it would taint her family name and image. One of the engineering students I interviewed even went to the extreme of saying, "A girl from a good family wouldn't work with men." He was opposed by other students who believed that it was merely a question of time before this idea would become socially acceptable. The middle classes hold the same view, although there are a few women from this class who work with men. This class's attitude is based on its strong drive to affiliate itself with the upper class. For the lower class of people, which does not necessarily mean poor, but rather families who are not socially "important", the problem is of less consequence.

In the medical profession, female nurses and doctors are greatly needed for female care and treatment. In 1966, the School of Nursing was established to meet this need, and the teaching is carried out in English. The course lasts four years, and students are only accepted after sitting interviews and provided they have attained the educational standards required. The students are sent abroad for six months (mostly to Ireland), so that they can acquire a working knowledge of English. The graduates of the School of Nursing immediately qualify for a job at the Hamad Hospital, Rumaillah Hospital, or the Women's Hospital. At the Ministry of Public Health, where 112 Qatari women are employed, we find more female nurses taking care of male patients and working with male doctors. Even in the women's hospital, total segregation is not enforced, as nurses work with male doctors and mix frequently with male visitors. In the ultrasonic scanning section, a female Qatari doctor receives male patients. Some Qatari women who work as doctors believe that society's attitudes are slowly changing in this respect.

'Aisha Al Kawari was the first female Qatari paediatrician to work at the Hamad Hospital, although she is now pursuing her studies in the United States. Aisha studied medicine in Cairo, despite the strong objection of the older male members of her family. "My mother came with me, and the problem was solved." She spoke on the radio, encouraging young women to participate in other spheres of knowledge and help their country. A very quiet, composed and humble person, she said she had chosen her specialization because she loved children. "It is a challenge to work with children, because they must like you first before you can do anything with them." On working Qatari women, she had this to say: "If they are convinced that what they are doing is right, why are they ashamed to voice their opinion? Obviously, education is not enough. You find some highly educated women who voice some strong opinions on changing their status, and these are sometimes the worst advocates of their own cause. They are supposed to be broadminded, but refuse to speak on radio, television, or even in newspapers. They won't have their pictures taken or do anything positive. I'm not saying that talking to the media is the only solution, but it certainly helps to portray the new image of young women. In the past, the woman's voice was not to be heard, either on radio or anywhere else. But now the social attitudes have changed . . . now it's what you say and how you say it that counts."

'Aisha Al Kawari worked with men at hospital, studied with them at Cairo University, and believes there are certain rules to be followed by every girl if she wants to avoid public scrutiny. She wears a long skirt, long sleeves and a black headscarf. "Well, I know that as long as I behave in a respectable way and concentrate on my profession, there's no problem. Of course, when you work with men, people criticize you at first, but later on they will realize they were wrong, and that working with men was just part of what you wanted to do . . . your job." With a deep understanding of her society and a dignified awareness of women's role within their society, 'Aisha is an authentic person who does what she believes is right and maintains her respectability as well as her colleagues' high esteem.

The early seventies witnessed several changes which opened new doors for Qatari women in the job market. These basically centred on the Government's investments in industry, which accelerated the pace of development, and the growing influence of the media in providing women with the chance of knowing more about world issues. The move into, for example, the oil industry and information work was not sudden and was not undertaken by many women, but it did serve the purpose of making working with men more acceptable by social standards. The pioneers in these fields better reflect such a trend. One of my interviewees who wasn't interested in teaching was unable to seek any other job at the time (1964), because of her family's strong opposition and society's attitudes. Later on, when more women had begun working with men and she was married with two children, she was allowed to take a secretarial job. She worked as the principal secretary of the Civil Aviation College.

Hissa Al Jaber graduated in Civil Engineering from Kuwait University but despite her great desire to work as an engineer, her parents wouldn't allow her to be the first to work in an exclusively men's occupation in Qatar.

Hissa was an active member of the Women's Branch of the Qatar Red Crescent Society and worked at the Hamad Hospital before leaving for the United States to pursue her studies.

"I'm working in the computer department of the Hamad Hospital but that isn't what I really want to do ... you see I've always loved engineering, since schooldays, and I know I can be a good engineer and contribute something to my country ... only then my family and the whole society will realize that engineering is not really for men only." According to

Hissa, most sections of Qatari society do not respect girls who work with men. Her family, however, did not object to her working with men at Hamad Hospital nor to her travelling abroad to pursue her studies.

Qatar Radio first began broadcasting in 1968, and, initially, women's participation was totally unacceptable and much criticized. Nonetheless, 'Aisha Hassan was the first Qatari girl to work as an announcer, joining the radio in its infancy. In the early seventies, more female Qatari announcers joined the Broadcasting Service, and by the mid-seventies there were four altogether, in addition to an increasing number in other sections of the Ministry of Information.

'Aisha is now head of the women's programmes section, and produces a daily half-hour edition of the woman's programme. "I try to enlighten my audience and I take into consideration that I'm speaking to a variety of nationalities. But the Qatari woman remains my basic concern." Through her programmes, 'Aisha tries to eradicate superstitious beliefs like those related to widowhood, and to correct misconceptions about women's religious rights. "For the more educated women, I have translated articles that inform them of women's activities around the world, and I regularly interview women from the Women's Branch of the Qatari Red Crescent Society or the Social Affairs Department. As for the less educated, I provide basic information on childcare, health, etc." She realizes the important part her programmes can play in helping women, especially as her audience is a large one.

On the administrative level, 'Aisha takes part in official meetings to discuss policy-making and other matters related to broadcasting. She was sent abroad to Britain and the United States to obtain a close view of broadcasting techniques. In the same context, she also visited Jordan, Kuwait, the United Arab

Emirates and Bahrain. "My father doesn't object to my travelling ... he did in the past before I worked for Qatar Radio, but I convinced him. My good reputation, and the respect of my colleagues proved I was right." 'Aisha certainly does not waste her time, and, apart from her duties and day-to-day radio commitments, is a student of English at the Language Institute. She goes to evening classes twice a week and will graduate later this year. She continues her job because she loves radio work and simply will not give it up.

On the other hand, there is the case of another ambitious young woman who worked as a part-time announcer in the Arabic service for nearly three years. She was studying English Literature at Qatar University and was very interested in the English Service. "Working with men is no problem, they are like my brothers, my family trusts me, and I know I can be respectable anywhere." When she finished her studies, I asked her if she would work full-time for radio, and she replied, "I don't think so." I never saw her afterwards, but I know that she gave up radio work after she married. Obviously, while marriage provides some women with more freedom in the choice of a job, it does restrict others. This is why marital status has a strong bearing on the numbers of women joining the work force, and why more divorced and single women work in traditionally male-dominated fields. The availability of jobs has encouraged most of them to remain unmarried. The single woman in the work force is a relatively new social factor, whose long-term effects on work patterns, social and female issues remain to be seen.

Some of the Qatari girls who work for the Qatar General Petroleum Corporation, QGPC, are employed in secretarial jobs. Zinah Al 'Attas works as the personnel manager's secretary. She thinks that working with men is no problem if the girl maintains the good reputation of her family. "My boss always encourages me, and his patience gives me a lot of support." With an incredibly good command of English, Zinah told me that she learnt a great deal when she was sent abroad (to Britain) with three other girls to take Secretarial English Language courses. Zinah's colleague, Mariam Al Ghadban, also mentioned the important boost given to women employed at QGPC by the deputy executive manager of offshore operations (a Qatari): "He tried his best to provide us with the chance to study here, then he sent us abroad. We went to a girls' college for 15 months in the UK. At first we were homesick, but we got used to it. However, we still prefer our own way of living." Both feel deep gratitude to the men whose guidance helped them in furthering their education and careers. As Mariam said, "We are proving to other girls that we can work with men ... there's no problem."

On the other hand, would Qatari men accept working for a female boss? From interviews carried out with engineering students at Qatar University, it transpired that most of them were against this idea. According to the visiting Professor of Sociology, Ayad Al Qazaz from California State University, "the question of domination of men is in every society, the difference is in the degree. Even in the United States where women have been participating in the work force for a long period of time, men still resent the idea of a woman being their boss. This generates great resentment and frustration on their part, resulting in tension and conflict between the female boss and the men." The reason for this is, as Professor Al Qazaz sees it, "the long history in which man was privileged, and it is difficult, especially in these societies, for man to give up his privileges and let himself be bossed by a woman". But, according to Mohammed 'Ali, the woman is in fact usually the boss: "I'm in this position; my boss at home is my wife, she plans my life. She's well educated, so I feel the ladies can be appointed to top management in certain places."

In short, there are still very few Qatari women who boss men; resistance to change, resentment and lack of cooperation often dominate their working relations. But some women's experiences have been successful so far.

The implications of women's employment for family and society

Once a Qatari woman starts work, she has to face a number of related problems concerning values and attitudes towards certain issues. Some of these issues concern the woman at work and others concern her as a mother and wife. Both reflect on society as they have a great bearing on the woman's productivity, and the size and stability of her family. The first set of problems concerns the choices a working woman has to make in order to maintain her "social credibility". In other words, should she pursue her career and be driven away from her social circle of acquaintances, or take a job which requires little if indeed any overtime, no travelling, etc? It may be hard for the Western reader to understand this, since in Europe, for example, women worked because of the economic need for them to add something to the family budget, regardless of working conditions and social ostracism. The problem of maintaining social credibility is of less consequence for a Qatari woman who works for shorter hours. Aminah Al Said's remarks elucidate this point quite admirably: "If the working woman cannot organize her time between work and leisure, she is in trouble. We're still a very close-knit society, and we care for each other. Friends simply must see each other once a week, and if one doesn't show up others may think they no longer want to come. Of course, we don't visit each other every day as our mothers did, but we do see each other once in a while."

This attitude is further supported by the availability of servants, who relieve women from the various laborious household chores. This should leave the woman enough free time to see her friends on a regular basis, even though some Qataris go to evening classes.

Psychologists have carried out lengthy studies and sometimes concluded that working women are frequently handicapped by a weak self-image and lack of self-confidence. In a study carried out in 1968, the American psychologist Martina Horner concluded that, as a result of their childhood training and various social pressures at home, many working women are hindered by a "fear of success", an acquired dread that the risk of succeeding is "loss of femininity". Qatari and Arab women in general greatly fear this loss of femininity, a social taboo. The reason for the absence of women in top management positions goes beyond the "fear-of-success" syndrome, and indeed some psychologists in the West have found that women's attitudes to work are totally different from men's, and these impede women's progress in a male-dominated world. Men, after all, tend to have long-term career goals, while women focus largely on short-term planning, as they have been brought up to think of careers conditionally – that is to say, as an alternative to marriage. The same can be said of most Qatari women, and most of my interviewees emphasized that they would give up work if they had to choose between earning a living and their family.

Work is considered by some women as a means of providing psychological relief, a compensation and recreation away from children and household activities, but according to Zinah Al 'Attas from QGPC, it is also much more than that. She believes that work provides women with a healthy opportunity to mix with other sectors of society and broaden the scope of their knowledge. Zinah sees work as more than a mere psychological relief; it is an experience that leaves a profound impression on a woman's personality. Mariam Al Ghadban, also from QGPC, wholeheartedly agrees: "Before I worked, I was extremely shy and afraid. Now I'm not. I'm no longer shy when I talk to people, especially to my male colleagues. Work has most definitely given me a lot of self-confidence."

On the other hand, other people may argue that work does not necessarily enhance the mental liberation of women. After all, a working woman more likely than not returns home exhausted, and her day is by no means finished as invariably she will have to prepare the meal, clean the house and take care of her children. This leaves very little time for reading and other intellectual pursuits.

Other problems can also hinder women's participation and efficiency in the labour force. The period of heaviest domestic responsibility occurs fairly early in a woman's work life, when apart from fulfilling her professional aspirations she also has to decide on the number of children she wants, find someone to look after them, and indeed decide whether to work or not during the childbearing and rearing period.

The short maternity leave of thirty days is not long enough for a mother to make her child secure and maintain breast-feeding. The media have been involved in a lengthy campaign promoting breast-feeding, in an effort to change the present trend of bottle-feeding, which is further encouraged by the mother's early return to work, leaving others to look after her child. Nevertheless, many mothers take leave without pay if the need arises.

Fawziah 'Abdul Wahid is a primary school teacher who had to leave her baby with a neighbour at first.

When she had a second child, she had to put both in a private nursery run by an unqualified housewife. The standard of health and care for the children was appalling, so her only alternative was to bring in an Indian nanny. But this only produces other problems, and Gulf sociologists are now expressing strong views against foreign nannies, believing that they exert a negative psychological and cultural influence on this generation of pre-school children. This would certainly appear to be true as many nannies come from extremely poor backgrounds, and more often than not are completely ignorant of basic health care. Invariably, their knowledge of Arabic and English is limited, sometimes non-existent, so the child is really being deprived of education and direction. The other negative factors occur when a nanny of a different religion, such as Buddhist, for example, spends most of her time with the child, and whether intentionally or not influences him by practising her religious rites in front of him. The language barrier also leaves the child confused and using non-Arabic words in his native language. This cultural influence is considered very serious in a society flooded with foreigners who all bring their different customs. (Gulf countries have long been subject to such influences and it is not surprising that English, Persian and Indian expressions which have been Arabized (e.g. *draiwel* is driver, *nikless* is necklace and so on), and even some Palestinian words and expressions are being used in the Gulf dialect.)

Finally, the presence of a full-time nanny who actually lives in the house means that the mother's sphere of influence and authority over her own children is limited. Instead of the mother sharing these with her mother-in-law, the nanny assumes a powerful position in the child's upbringing.

Tamader Ahmed is fortunate enough to be able to leave her children with her mother, which is still possible amongst those living within the extended family. Nevertheless, the younger generation of Qatari women are becoming more aware of the important role nurseries and kindergartens can play in educating children and encouraging them to be more creative at playtime. The Ministry of Education has already presented a draft resolution to the Advisory Council, pointing to the need for setting up nurseries financed by the government, on a modern basis. The kindergartens project stresses that nurseries should provide children with recreational and educational facilities, on lines similar to those of the British-run nurseries. They should discipline the child and provide proper health care facilities. In fact, the project is very ambitious and caters for nutrition and transportation and is to be executed in four stages. The whole project is still dormant, possibly because of its cost (the first stage alone is estimated to cost 130 million riyals), or because there are not enough available qualified Qatari teachers. Professor Wigdan Shami, a UNESCO expert who works at Qatar University, Home Economics Department, runs an experimental nursery where students are trained and acquire the necessary knowledge of children at pre-school level. She says: "The local nurseries were opened to provide a job for the people who run them, and who are mostly unqualified. But here we are preparing Qatari students to be able to deal with the child on a more scientific basis. Our aim is to provide sufficient numbers of pre-school teachers for the Ministry of Education."

The social repercussions resulting from facilitating women's entry into the labour market should also be taken into consideration at this juncture. In the United States, these produced adverse effects when some mothers left their children in day-care centres for eight to ten hours every day. Rising divorce rates and falling birth rates can also be attributed to the ever-increasing numbers of working women. This can also sow the seeds of dissent in the husband, who might feel insecure and resentful of a wife with a busy schedule, an income of her own, a position perhaps more prestigious than his and outside friendships and commitments.

In many Western societies, the arrival of the "two wage packet" family has been accompanied by a redefinition of family roles. Working women exercise a greater degree of power in their marriages, and the husbands now involve themselves slightly more in childcare and housework than they used to not long ago. Such changes can only be partially applied to the low-income family in Qatar and on the individual level. This is because most middle-class husbands can afford a maid, and simply do not concern themselves with a role they have been conditioned to avoid. These conclusions are based on general observation, as hitherto there has been no study of the effects of Qatari women entering the work force. In fact, much time and effort have been devoted to encouraging women to participate in greater numbers in the work force, as a vital contribution to the development process of their own country.

The role of Qatari women in development

The role of the woman in production, work and development has recently come to the forefront of discussions on women's status in any part of the world. The world plan of action, approved by the United Nations-sponsored population conference (1974), acknowledged the right of women to contribute to economic development and other activities, on an equal basis with men. 1975–85 has been designated by the UN as the decade for women, and two conferences were held in Mexico City (1975) and Copenhagen (1980), in which the international problems of women were discussed at length. There were some interesting differences of opinion between women from the advanced industrialized countries, and those from the developing areas of the world. The latter experienced difficulties in relating to Western women's demands (such as career opportunities), which separate a woman from her former social role. Women from developing countries were basically concerned with issues vital to their needs. The poorer countries argue that once world resources are re-structured, women in developing countries will immediately rise in status, after their countries have received their share of new wealth. The truth of this sentence can be felt in the different role Arab women play in the more developed Arab countries where industrialization forms the basis of its development schemes – Egypt and Iraq, for instance. There, women have entered new fields of employment, engineering and so on, which affect women's new-found status in the work force. The more women are needed and involved in the development process, the more social weight they are bound to carry and thus enhance their opportunities for promoting favourable change.

The richer countries of the developing world see the solution in implementing development pro-grammes. Feminist leaders from the West disagree, believing that economic development will continue to favour men. So while Western women recognize the role of the Industrial Revolution in promoting favourable social change, they refuse to acknowledge the potential role of development for Third World women in the same context.

Nevertheless, the developing areas, especially Gulf countries, have recently dedicated more regional conferences, seminars and studies to the issue of development and women's role in it. This is not only the result of increased awareness of the need to upgrade the status of women, but also a means of decreasing the dependence on migrant labour without hindering the development process. In a related article, which discussed the labour market performance in some Arab Gulf states and which was published in the book *Issues in Development: The Arab Gulf States*, Dr Henry T. Azzam explained: "For the present and near future, increasing dependence by the Gulf states on migrant labour is inevitable. Planners and policy makers in Kuwait, the United Arab Emirates and Qatar are becoming alarmed by the fact that expatriates constitute a majority in their countries, and disturbed by the thought that tensions and problems may arise as a consequence."

In a seminar held in Abu Dhabi in 1981 on the impact of oil on social change, a paper presented on the role of imported labour indicated that loyalty cannot be guaranteed. The imported labour is not integrated into the society, and thus its basic loyalty remains the profit motive. Moreover, most Gulf societies have been split into separate ethnic entities, more or less completely separated from each other socially and culturally where relationships are based on nationality. This is just one aspect of the problem which has led Gulf countries to make the entry and work conditions for imported labour more restrictive. But this problem should not reach greater proportions, as traditional exporters of labour into the region have almost reached the limit of their capacity to supply migrant labour.

Obviously, governments of Gulf countries are now faced with the challenge of mobilizing their human resources in the process of development. Dr Azzam has said, "Few nationals possess the skills needed in a modern economy, and the majority resist working in jobs they consider to be 'socially inferior'." This stems from an old traditional attitude where crafts and vocational work were looked down on, and were mostly undertaken by the newly integrated groups (Persians and Africans) in these societies. Of course, the problem of labour shortages is further aggravated by the non-wage income opportunities available to nationals. Dr Azzam stresses that "the various policies introduced by the governments of Gulf countries aiming to promote a more equitable distribution of income have in effect provided a sort of 'economic rent' for nationals, and made it possible for them to resist work in the modern sector and substitute for it self-styled employment."

The same could be said regarding women, where social welfare policies have eliminated women's economic need to work. In most developing countries such policies were implemented following women's entry into the labour market. In the Gulf area, they were introduced before the majority of potential labour, men and women, entered the work force. In an indirect way, the governments' generosity has affected negatively women's entry into the job market; whilst a man has to be unable to work in order to qualify for social welfare, the woman is entitled to her allowance even if she is able to work. However, from a sequence of articles published in UAE newspapers on whether women prefer to live on social welfare allowances instead of earning their own living, most preferred not having to work.

In the overall development process, vocational training in broader spheres could help in utilizing women who have only had a small amount of education. One sociologist in a seminar on the impact of oil on Arab societies commented: "What are the guarantees provided for childhood? We are asking women to leave home and children and go out to work to help in development schemes. We're also asking them not to rely on Indian and foreign nannies because of the negative repercussions on society as a whole but we haven't provided an alternative yet. Are there enough nurseries, or are we going to establish government-funded nurseries for working mothers? I personally believe that if the Gulf woman is more productive at home and will bring up a generation, that can contribute to development. Let her do just that."

Women who participated in the Second Regional Conference on Gulf Women feel rather differently about the subject. They believe that sex-labelling of occupational fields should be eliminated, in addition to eradicating illiteracy and providing better work conditions by increasing nurseries and childcare centres. Only then can indigenous Gulf female labour take over from the expatriates.

Finally, Qatari women's role in development was not haphazardly chosen to conclude this preliminary effort to portray a more realistic image of Qatari women. The choice was intended to leave the reader with one important question: are there indications that the future of Qatari women will be better than the present? The answer really lies in what has been said throughout the book by Qatari men and women.

Bibliography

Books

ABD AL 'ATI, HAMMUDAH   *Islam in Focus*. American Trust Publications, 1975

        The Family Structure in Islam. American Trust Publications, 1977

AL 'AKKAD, SALAH   *Political Currents in the Arab Gulf*. Anglo Library, Egypt, 1974

AL A'SAR, SAFA   *Psychological studies of Qatari Society*. Anglo Library, Egypt, 1978

ARNOLD, SIR THOMAS W.   *Painting in Islam*. Dover Publications Inc., New York, 1965

DAFTARI, MAY ZIWAR   *Issues in Development: The Arab Gulf States*. MD Research and Services Ltd., 1980

AL DOWAIK, M. TALIB SALMAN   *The Popular Song in Qatar*. (4 parts). Ministry of Information Publications, Qatar, 1975

DOZY, REINHART   *Dictionnaire des noms des vêtements chez les Arabes*. Amsterdam, 1845

HUSSEIN, TAHYA KAMEL   *History and Evolution of Costumes*. Nahdat Misr, 1960

AL ISSA, JOHAINA   *Modernisation in Contemporary Qatari Society*. Kathma, Kuwait, 1979

AL IZZI, NAJLA   "Silver and Golden Jewellery", *Treasures of Qatar National Museum*. Vol 2. Ministry of Information Publications, Qatar, 1983

JABER & EL SHEIKH   *Psychological Studies of The Arab Character*. 'Alam Al Kutub, Cairo, 1978

AL JADIR, SAOUD   *Arab and Islamic Silver*. Stacey International, 1981

KAMAL, SAFWAT   *A Preliminary Study of Kuwaiti Folklore*. Kuwaiti Government Press, 1974
Customs and Traditions of Marriage in Kuwait. Kuwaiti Government Press, 1974

AL KATHEMI, Z. KATHEM   *Excerpts from the Folklore of the Arab Gulf and Arabian Peninsula*. Al Basra University, 1981

KHALIFAH 'ALI ABDULLAH   *Poetry of Ibn Farhan*. Ministry of Information Publications, Qatar, 1980

AL KHOSOSI, BADR EDDIN ABBAS   *Studies in the Current History of the Arab Gulf*. Zat Al Salasil, Kuwait, 1978

KHOURI, M.A. & AL GAR, HAMID   *An Anthology of Modern Arabic Poetry*. University of California Press, 1974

LINTON, RALPH.   *The Study of Man*. D. Appleton – Century Inc., New York, 1936

MAKHLOUF, CARLA   *Changing Veils: Women and Modernisation in North Yemen*. University of Texas Press, 1979

MA'SOUMI, GHOLAM RIZA   *Siraf (Bandar Tahri)*. Silislat Intisharat, Iran, 1962

MAYER, L.A.   *Mamlouk costumes*. Kundig, Geneva, 1952

MELIKIAN, LEVON   *Oil and Social Change in the Arab world*. The Arab Planning Institute, Kuwait, 1976

AL NASERI, M. 'ALI   *Popular Proverbs of the Gulf Area*. Al Mushrik, Beirut, 1981

RICE, DAVID TALBOT   *Islamic Art*. Thames and Hudson, 1975

ROBERTS, ROBERT   *The Social Laws of the Qoran*. Williams and Norgate Ltd, 1925

ROSS, HEATHER COLYER   *Bedouin Jewellery in Saudi Arabia*. Stacey International, 1978

AL RUMAIHI, M. GHANEM   *Oil and Social Change in the Arabian Gulf*. Al-Wehda, Kuwait, 1975

Factors Hindering Economic and Social Developments of Contemporary Gulf Societies. Kathma, Kuwait, 1977

SOFFAN, LINDA USRA. *The Women of the United Arab Emirates*. Croom Helm, London, 1980

SPACKS, PATRICIA MEYER *The Female Imagination*. Alfred A. Knopf Inc., 1975

AL SALIM, HIDAYAT SULTAN *Papers of a Traveller in the Arabian Gulf*. Kuwait Government, 1969

EL SHAARWI, SHEIKH MOHAMMED *Islam and Contemporary Thought: Four Public Lectures*. QNP Press, 1976

AL SHAMLAN & SEIF MARZOOQ *History of Pearl Diving in Kuwait and the Arabian Gulf*. Kuwait Government Press, Part 1 1975, Part 2 1978

WADDY, CHARIS *Women in Muslim History*. Longman, 1980

WESTERMARCK, EDWARD ALEXANDER. *The History of Human Marriage*. 3 vols. The Allerton Book Co., New York, 1922.

WILSON, SIR ARNOLD T. *The Arabian Gulf*. (Arabic translation.) Al A'mal, Kuwait, 1962

ZAHLAN, ROSEMARIE SAID *The Creation of Qatar*. Harper and Row, Publishers Inc., 1979

Journals

"The Women's Movement", *Editorial Research Reports. Congressional Quarterly Inc*. USA, 1977

Al-Fikr Al-Arabi. Vols 17 & 18. Arab Development Institute, Tripoli 1980

Journal of Gulf and Arabian Peninsula Studies. Vol 1. No.4 1975 – Vol 4 No.14 1980

Al-Mustaqbal Al-Arabi. Vol 1 1981 – Vol 3 1983 Centre
  for Arab Unity Studies

Oil and Social Change in the Arab World. Arab
  Planning Institute, Kuwait, 1981

Studies on Kuwaiti and Gulf Women's Status.
  Women's Social and Cultural Society in Kuwait,
  1976

Newspapers and magazines

In Qatar   *Al Doha* magazine (1979–)
                Al Rayyah newspaper (1980–)
                Al 'Oroba magazine (1972–1980)
                Al Jawhra (1981–)

In the United Arab Emirates   *Zahrat Al-Khaleeg*
  (1980–)

In Saudi Arabia   *Sayidaty.* Vol 2. Jedda, 1982